WEEDING THROUGH THE BS
From Idea To Acquisition

Steven G. Edwards

The author generated the cover image in part with Dall-E.

www.innovativeinkpublishing.com
Send all inquiries to:
4050 Westmark Drive
Dubuque, IA 52004-1840

Print ISBN: 979-8-7657-9759-4
Ebook ISBN: 979-8-7657-9760-0

Published in the United States of America

Dedication

To my dearest Wife Christine, our resilient children, my valued business partner, dedicated team members, supportive mentors, and believing customers:

This book is dedicated to each of you for the pivotal roles you played in the creation and success of our business. Your unwavering support and belief in my dreams and endeavors have been the driving force behind every late night, every challenging decision, and every step forward.

To my beloved wife, who stood by my side when I declared my commitment to this venture, your love and understanding have been my anchor through every storm, and your strength has been my constant source of inspiration.

To our remarkable children, who endured the chaos of a father launching a new company and those sleepless nights, your resilience and understanding have taught me the true meaning of balance and purpose.

To my trusted business partner Gary, who shared my vision and had faith in my ideas, your collaboration and dedication have turned dreams into reality.

To the incredible team members at Premier Virtual, both past and present, your hard work and dedication have been the bricks in the foundation of our success. Your contributions are woven into the very fabric of this company.

To my invaluable mentors, who offered guidance and wisdom when I needed it most, your insights and encouragement have been my North Star.

And to our cherished customers, who believed in our software platform, your trust and support have driven us to constantly improve and innovate.

This book is a testament to the power of collective effort, unwavering faith, and the strength that can be found in unity. Without each and every one of you, this journey would have been incomplete. My gratitude knows no bounds, and this dedication is a humble acknowledgment of your immeasurable contributions.

With deepest appreciation and love,
Steven G. Edwards

Contents

"Steve is a very genuine business founder and entrepreneur who possesses an immense amount of practical experience and knowledge for both today's business owners and those in the future."

Kevin Cox—Director of FAU's Adams Center for Entrepreneurship
Senior Entrepreneurship Instructor, Bootcamp, Tech Runway Accelerator, NSF I-Corps
Department of Management, College of Business, FAU

Steve Edwards walks the walk when it comes to living the entrepreneurial dream. From bootstrap to successful acquisition, he "weeds through the BS" and tells it like it is. This book is a must read for any leader who wants to level up. Same goes for Steve's Ted Talk: he leads by example and shares great tips and takeaways about building a successful corporate culture!

Cindy Metzler—President at Omm Media

Steve's innovative thinking and fresh perspectives offer a transformative approach to the subject, casting new light on established ideas.

Jessica Beaver—Associate Director FAU Tech Runway

Steve's story is a great example of what can happen when you think outside the box, put in the hard work, and have a never-give-up attitude, from day one! It can literally make the stars align, and boy did they!

John Morgan—Founder and Managing Member at Connected Consultants

---

The author's honest and transparent presentation of his real world business startup experience makes this book a must read for anyone considering, or in the startup process. His views regarding mentoring provide invaluable insights and advice for those in or entering a business-mentoring program.

Scott Barlass—Leader Journey Professionals—Christ Centered Business Ministry

---

The author fearlessly navigates truth, delivering a candid and direct perspective that cuts through pretense and offers raw, invaluable insights, setting a refreshing tone of unfiltered honesty.

Jason Hill—Founder of Owwll App—Host of The Shrimp Tank Boca Raton

---

Introduction

In the world of entrepreneurship, the journey from inception to acquisition is often viewed through a romanticized lens, highlighting the successes, the glory, and the riches. But this book, penned by a true entrepreneur who bootstrapped their company from an idea to acquisition, peels back the layers to reveal a raw and unfiltered account of the struggle, the ups and downs, and the sheer tenacity required to build a business from the ground up.

Here, you will not find a fairy tale of overnight success, nor a blueprint for guaranteed prosperity. Instead, you will find the essence of the entrepreneurial spirit—the essence of what it means to take an idea, to believe in it wholeheartedly, and to face every obstacle, every setback, and every moment of doubt head-on.

The author's story is a testament to resilience, resourcefulness, and unwavering determination. In these pages, they share the unvarnished truth about the trials and tribulations that come with entrepreneurship. The late nights, the lonely decisions, the financial woes, and the sleepless moments of existential questioning—all of it laid bare for you, the aspiring entrepreneur, to witness and learn from.

But this book is not just about the struggle. It's about the unquenchable fire that burns within those who dare to defy the odds. It's about the lessons learned from failures, the resilience forged in adversity, and the triumph that follows relentless effort. It's a story that encapsulates the emotional rollercoaster every entrepreneur endures, a rollercoaster that brings equal parts frustration and exhilaration.

So, whether you are just starting on your entrepreneurial journey or you've already embarked on the path of business creation, this book is a compass, guiding you through the labyrinth of entrepreneurship. It is a reminder that the entrepreneurial dream is attainable but comes with no shortcuts. It's a call to action, urging you to persist, adapt, and thrive.

As you delve into these pages, remember that every business, just like this book, begins with an idea. And every successful entrepreneur, just like the author, starts with a vision, fueled by passion and determination. Embrace the story, savor the wisdom, and let it serve as a source of inspiration and guidance on your own entrepreneurial odyssey.

This book is a testament to the fact that the journey is as valuable as the destination. The entrepreneur's path is not for the faint of heart, but it is one filled with unparalleled opportunities for growth and success. So, with this knowledge in hand, dare to dream, dare to create, and dare to build. May this book be your trusted companion as you embark on your own entrepreneurial voyage. Bon voyage!

Steven G. Edwards

Is This Really Happening?

The Venture Capital Meeting

I was introduced to a local Venture Capital (VC) firm, and they wanted to hear our pitch. A buddy of mine called in a favor to speak directly with the head of the firm instead of going through the normal process, which I will talk about later in the book. At this point we were thinking about raising capital and this looked like a great opportunity. The call was set up with him (we will call him Jon), myself, and my CFO (Bryan). We're going through the pitch deck and Jon tells me that he did his research on my firm before we got on the call. He tells me that he understands our business, the problem we are trying to solve, our market strategy, and our competition!

Now, I'm thinking I'm in front of an educated investor who will immediately jump at the opportunity to invest.

But I couldn't have been more wrong! Jon proceeds to tell me that he's got a buddy that's in my industry and that he called him asking about us. He said his buddy never heard of us and that kind of worried him. Well, no shit, we had just launched. Realization #1: A title on a business card doesn't make you an expert.

So, we took a look at his buddy's website, and I realized that it has nothing to do with the problem we were solving and couldn't have been farther away from what our software did. I calmly and carefully explained our differences, but Jon became arrogant and pushed back hard. I had to recall all of my mentoring and military discipline to not leap across the table. I kept my cool and left with my dignity intact but disappointed that while I was pitch perfect, I was pitching to a wall.

Realization #2—Make sure you qualify your potential investor—by determining if they are investing at your level and in your industry.

After the call I was seething and had to blow off the steam that had accumulated during the pitch.

So, I called my CFO and told him, "I don't care if Jon wants to write me a check for US$10 million I'll decline it and not do business with him". I'm looking for "smart" money, that can provide not only dollars but advice and connections.

You may ask, how could I be so confident in my encounter with venture capitalists that are supposedly investment experts. I credit it to my military training and my pitch preparation provided by The Venture Mentoring Team. They prepared me for this worst-case scenario and for so much more.

But this was not my first "meat grinder" event. The first, believe it or not, came from one of my greatest assets, my mentors.

Meeting my future mentors

It's October of 2019, before anyone really heard of virtual events and there certainly was no crying need for a virtual event.

Reflecting on that organization, my mentor team, and my pitch preparation, I gained insight into how people viewed my business, how to respond to questions, and how best to explain our company. It opened my eyes to perspectives that investors might fail to grasp. Although I felt defeated and disheartened internally, my unwavering belief in my idea and company persisted. To this day, I maintain a relationship with those mentors and can reach out to them whenever needed.

The Pitch Scrub

The phone rang, and I promptly answered. It was Bob from The Venture Mentoring Team informing me that I had reached the final stages of the application process for their mentoring program. The application process had been lengthy, and Bob called to schedule a pitch scrub, which served as the final step to determine if I had met their criteria.

Bob explained that the scrub was an opportunity to present my pitch and to gain insight on how to improve my pitch, my business, and to gain not one, but a team of mentors.

On the day of the pitch, I woke up with a heightened sense of confidence. I prepared myself, exuding more swagger than usual, knowing that I was about to enter the room and captivate everyone with my brilliant idea. I imagined they would readily embrace my plan and acknowledge its flawless execution. It was a sunny day in South Florida as I entered the conference room, where six professional executives awaited my arrival. Surveying the room, I sought out friendly faces in the crowd to focus my attention on. The room was evenly divided between men and women, and it appeared that they all wore smiles. Little did I know, that my swagger would betray me and that I was stepping into a challenging situation.

These individuals hailed from Corporate Development, seasoned business executives whose companies had been acquired for millions, and current founders of successful enterprises. As I set up my laptop with the meticulously crafted pitch deck I had spent countless hours perfecting, there was minimal conversation directed at me. However, I couldn't help but notice the whispering among themselves. At first glance, it seemed like an easy pitch—their smiles reassured me of my own confidence. I believed this day would be a turning point in my life. I introduced myself, presented my idea, and that's when I realized the magnitude of the task before me.

I started my pitch, and went through the first slide, my problem statement. Instantly, they began questioning me, was there really a problem to solve, was there a market, why was I the guy to solve it and why was I the one to bring it to market. I indicated that I would address their concerns shortly, but they insisted on an immediate response. Beads of sweat formed on my forehead, yet I remained steadfast, refusing to let them see my unease. I delved into the problem I aimed to solve, but they persisted with their inquiries. They questioned the very existence of the problem and doubted my understanding of it. In that moment, I began to wonder whether this was truly a problem or if they simply failed to comprehend its significance.

What I found out later was that, like in the military, force is met with force. My approach, my demeanor, and especially my swagger indicated that I could take their strongest critique. I also later discovered that if I had come looking for advice and guidance I would have been treated much differently.

As I glanced around the room, I noticed a few individuals who seemed to grasp the problem, but not all shared the same understanding. I explained that my expertise stemmed from over nine years of experience in the job fair industry, during which I witnessed a decline in event attendance. One mentor proceeded to question the source of my expertise in that field, deeming my nine-year tenure insufficient evidence. As I moved to the next slide, the onslaught of questions continued, accompanied by countless headshakes expressing disbelief. It felt as though nothing I said could quell their doubts.

Nevertheless, I persevered, progressing through slide after slide. Halfway through the presentation, I felt defeated in my mind, and even as I write this, I find myself squeezing a stress ball, recalling the ordeal. Yet, I cannot help but smile when I reflect on the outcome. I questioned myself once more—was this truly a good idea? Did I possess the necessary qualities to succeed? Was I truly an expert? These individuals grilled me like I had never been grilled before.

A flashback to my basic training days crossed my mind, where a drill sergeant would yell at me while I performed pushups. For a brief moment, I contemplated whether I would rather return to that scenario. But I swiftly snapped back to reality, recognizing that I was indeed an expert. I possessed extensive knowledge of the industry, and most importantly, I firmly believed in my astounding idea. I refused to let individuals seemingly unfamiliar with my industry deter me from pursuing my plans. After all, I had parachuted from airplanes despite my fear of heights—no one could hinder me from executing my intentions.

Admittedly, there were many aspects of the business world and establishing a tech startup as a nontech founder that eluded me. However, deep within my heart and mind, I held unwavering faith that I was the one capable of making it work. So, I raised my voice and exuded even greater confidence. "I AM THE EXPERT," I proclaimed, elucidating why I would triumph. Yet, this only elicited more questions, as they endeavored to undermine my confidence and spirit.

Their objective was to break me, but I refused to succumb. I pressed on, pitching my audacious idea that would revolutionize recruiting. This was a pre-COVID-19 concept that had yet to gain significant attention. However, their responses conveyed negativity, and their skepticism began to infiltrate my thoughts. What I came to realize was this team was preparing me for the reality of investor presentations. It was startup basic training.

At one point, Roger, one of the mentors interjected, "Steve, you're doing great. Keep it up." It was the first positive comment I had heard in what felt like an eternity. That day seemed interminable, surpassing even the duration of an overnight birth with my sons. However, I later discovered that the experience was not entirely negative. Their intention was to test my coachability, provoking me to see how I would respond. While I felt that I should have been forewarned, I recognized that such knowledge may have diminished the impact.

What I Learned about Dealing with Investors

Subsequently, I learned valuable lessons from that experience when dealing with investors. In fact, they had been relatively lenient with me. That encounter left a lasting impression, teaching me to maintain confidence in my ideas, resist the influence of negativity and self-doubt, and above all, acknowledge that they were present to assist me on my journey. Roger eventually became my lead mentor, and we will discuss him and the program in greater detail later.

Finally, the pitch scrub concluded after an hour, although it felt considerably longer. Have you ever experienced a situation where every word you uttered seemed wrong? That was precisely how I felt. Although that sensation was genuine, there was more to the situation than met the eye. In reality, they had provided me with valuable insights and commendations. However, a part of me felt somewhat defeated. Their feedback contained invaluable advice that still resonates with me today.

Their aim was to help me and witness my success. Not everyone is accepted into this program, so they wanted to ensure that I was genuinely deserving. Countless individuals possess ideas, but few truly comprehend what it takes to achieve success. It was an immensely enlightening experience.

Then, something occurred that shook me. Still on edge, I overheard two women conversing. One of them glanced in my direction and remarked, "I don't even like the name of your company. Why would you choose something like that?" I remained silent, brushing off the comment. I endured the jabs and criticisms, nearly succumbing to a knockout blow, but this particular comment struck a nerve.

Interestingly, it was my wife who had suggested the name when we were exploring potential company names. Instantly, I lost respect for that person. Their comment, unrelated to the pitch scrub, felt highly disrespectful. In the subsequent events, I made certain decisions that may or may not have been the right ones. However, I unwaveringly believed in my company, its product, and its name. We will delve into that story a bit later.

Exiting the pitch scrub, I felt as though I had just gone twelve rounds with Mike Tyson. (Or maybe one round and he knocked me out!) I called my business partner and expressed, "I need a drink. I've never been beaten up like this before in my life."

What I Learned about the Pitch Scrub

This pitch scrub served a couple of purposes. Firstly, it aimed to determine whether the organization would accept me into their mentoring program and if my idea had the potential to succeed. Secondly, the pitch scrub assessed my coachability—how well I handled criticism and feedback. Did I accept it gracefully or argue against every point raised?

Initially, I failed to grasp the significance of the pitch scrub. However, it would prove invaluable later in my career. Despite the grueling questioning and the deluge of negativity, I never became frustrated. I maintained composure, refraining from raising my voice or offering any form of retort. I remained confident and true to myself. This demeanor led to my acceptance into their program, where I gained six mentors eager to guide and support me.

Yet, I made another misstep. I sent an email to the entire group, expressing gratitude for their time and the valuable questions and insights they had shared. However, I included a statement I shouldn't have. At the bottom of the email, I wrote, "If you're here to volunteer your time and provide constructive and productive input that can help my business progress, I would love to have you on my team. But if you're here to criticize and condemn the name of my company, I don't want you as a mentor." Then, I clicked the send button.

The Aftermath

Shortly after, my phone buzzed. It was Bob, and he was concerned. He provided guidance on how I should have handled the situation better. Due to my email, some mentors began to doubt my coachability, perceiving a hint of attitude. Consequently, the mentor in question and another mentor who had engaged in the name discussion withdrew their mentorship. I remained unfazed by their departure, as the four mentors who remained proved invaluable to me and my business.

I share this story not to discourage or dissuade you, but to emphasize the value of mentors and their ability to assist you. As I have mentioned numerous times before, mentor groups play a pivotal role in the success of any new startup, particularly those lacking comprehensive knowledge. One might perceive this narrative as excessively negative, but in the end, it proved to be an incredibly positive learning experience that I believe everyone should go through. Especially if one intends to approach investors or seek funding, as this is precisely how they will scrutinize and challenge you.

Investors can find countless reasons to invest in you, but they need just one reason to decline. Therefore, every interaction with your mentors becomes a valuable lesson. Now, let's dive deep into how I arrived at this point and explore the challenges of a tech startup as a nontech founder.

To Sum Things Up

The pitch scrub served two purposes: determining acceptance into the mentoring program and evaluating my coachability. Initially, I didn't fully grasp its significance, but I was later told that I maintained composure and confidence throughout, leading to my acceptance. However, I made a misstep by sending an email expressing gratitude by including an inappropriate statement. Some mentors doubted my coachability, resulting in the withdrawal of two mentors. Reflecting on the experience, I gained insight into how my business is perceived and the value of mentorship. Mentor teams are crucial for startup success, and their feedback prepares you for investor scrutiny. Every interaction with mentors brings a valuable lesson.

1. **The importance of confidence**: Enter the pitch scrub with a heightened sense of confidence, believing in the brilliance of your idea. Confidence can help in delivering a compelling pitch and standing firm in the face of challenging questions. But too much swagger can be detrimental.

2. **Dealing with skepticism**: You will face skepticism and intense questioning from both mentors and investors. The mentor experience will teach you the importance of preparing for tough questions, addressing concerns effectively, and maintaining composure even when faced with doubt.

3. **Resilience in the face of adversity**: Despite feeling defeated and enduring criticism, persevere and refuse to let negativity or self-doubt hinder their determination. The lesson here is to stay resilient and not let setbacks discourage you from pursuing your goals.

4. **Recognizing valuable feedback**: Realize that the mentor team's intention is not to break you but to test your coachability and provide valuable insights. It is essential to approach feedback with an open mind, recognizing that it can help refine and improve your ideas.

5. **Selecting the right mentors**: Make the decision to prioritize mentors who were supportive and aligned with your vision, even if it means letting go of mentors who had differing opinions. Choosing mentors who genuinely understand and believe in your business can be crucial for success.

6. **Learning from mentorship experiences**: Acknowledge the value of mentor teams and the role they play in guiding and supporting startups. This highlights the importance of seeking out mentors who can provide expertise, guidance, and constructive feedback.

7. **The impact of communication**: The email following the pitch scrub had unintended consequences, causing some mentors to question my coachability. This lesson emphasizes the significance of effective and thoughtful communication, particularly when interacting with mentors and stakeholders.

8. **Understanding investor scrutiny**: The pitch scrub experience can mirror how investors scrutinize and challenge entrepreneurs seeking funding. This underscores the importance of being prepared for investor interactions and being able to address their concerns effectively.

9. **The value of a diverse mentor team**: Despite the challenges faced, maintain a relationship with the mentors whose guidance you find to be valuable. This highlights the benefits of having a mentor team with diverse perspectives and expertise that can provide a well-rounded support network.

Overall, the lessons learned are about confidence, resilience, responding to skepticism, seeking valuable feedback, selecting the right mentors, effective communication, investor scrutiny, and the value of a diverse mentor team from the author's experience with a pitch scrub and mentorship program.

The Aha Moment and the Birth of Premier Virtual

Every good idea is met with criticism, but those who criticize may be uninformed or unaware of the potential of your idea. Every successful business started as a mere concept, just like a tree started as a nut and every flower started as a seed. Amazon, Google, Facebook, and Uber were once startups that began with an idea, executed it, gained traction, and look at where they are today.

Despite the naysayers and skeptics who claim your idea won't work or isn't good enough, its important to believe in your idea. Do you believe it has the potential to change someone's life? Do you believe you can do something unique that nobody else is doing? Even if your idea is in an existing market, are you improving upon it or adding a unique twist?

The Birth of Premier Virtual

After organizing in-person job fairs for nine years, I noticed a shift in the market. Attendance started to decline as people preferred applying for jobs online rather than waiting in line at job fairs. In 2017, the in-person job fair industry I was in was dying, and I needed to make a change.

The Inspiration

Around that time, a mentor of mine landed a new client involved in virtual reality events. They mentioned the idea of virtual job fairs to me, which was still in its early stages. Intrigued, I wanted to explore the possibilities. They showed me a demo of a platform, and I immediately realized that this was the future of job fairs. However, the cost was prohibitive and did not make financial sense to me at the time.

I urged that organization to go back to the drawing board and come back with better pricing. We scheduled a meeting for the following week. During this time, I started envisioning the potential of virtual job fairs. With the in-person job fairs, I had to travel from one market to another, spending days away from home and my family. It was a demanding and exhausting schedule that I wanted to leave behind. The concept of virtual job fairs offered the opportunity for regional and statewide events without the need for travel. This realization brought immense joy to my wife and children, as it meant I could be present with them more often.

The following week, we reconvened with the vendor over the phone. To my surprise, he presented the same pricing but offered more virtual booths. It became apparent that he was merely showcasing another company's software. Intrigued, I conducted research on that company and its competitors, scheduling demos on their platforms. Interestingly, I learned that the vendor that I was communicating with didn't even have the right to demonstrate the platform he had shown me! The vendor had merely done a demo with them and would only purchase if I signed an agreement with him.

The Announcement

After carefully reviewing all the platforms, I chose the one I was going to go with. I chose the platform that was not only the most affordable but also a new company willing to collaborate with us.

I approached the owner of the company I had a license with for in-person events and proposed the idea of transitioning to virtual events. We both invested US$5,000 each for three events, intending to run simultaneous virtual events in Florida and New Jersey, an approach that had not been done before.

When discussing the concept with my clients, I had to provide thorough explanations of how virtual events worked, and they embraced the idea. However, the NJ market showed less enthusiasm. As a result, we decided to focus solely on running events in Florida, dividing them regionally throughout the state. These virtual events proved to be successful, solidifying my belief that this was the direction to pursue going forward.

While we maintained a cordial relationship with the organization in New Jersey, we eventually parted ways as they remained firm in their preference for in-person events and were not receptive to the virtual approach. However, we remain friends to this day and continue to discuss industry trends and ongoing changes. Technology is transforming the recruitment landscape and will continue to do so. As I always say, someone will inevitably come up with a new mouse trap that catches on. Just look at how Monster, then CareerBuilder, Indeed, and Zip Recruiter all revolutionized the way recruitment and job boards were approached.

After successfully running three events on the virtual platform, we decided to sign a larger annual agreement. However, that's when we encountered problems, and we realized that we were expecting a significant amount of work from the vendor for very little compensation. They were a fairly new platform in the virtual space at the time and we were changing the way they did things. They expressed their unwillingness to continue working with our events and kindly let us out of our agreement. While they were a great organization, our demands were quite high. This led us to search for a new virtual vendor.

The Big Risk Taker

We selected the next vendor, and they presented us with a ten-page plus agreement. Our attorney reviewed it and informed us that it had certain limitations that could pose issues if we ever wanted to build our own platform. This conversation sparked discussions with Gary, and we began exploring the idea of developing our own platform to host our events. I believed I had a more efficient and effective way to build and operate it. But, as a nontech founder, had to navigate the complexities of founding a tech company and the struggles of starting a business from scratch without any experience or knowledge in tech.

As my vision differed from what was currently being done in the field, Premier Virtual was born out of necessity.

The Life of an Entrepreneur

THE WORK HOURS

So many people talk about work-life balance, but what does that really mean for an entrepreneur? When it comes to work-life balance, people often have different perceptions, especially for entrepreneurs. I frequently encounter the assumption that as an entrepreneur, I must be working between 18 and 20 hours a day. And I just look at the people that ask me that, and say to them, does that make sense? I love my wife, kids, and my family. I love to spend time with them. Part of the reason I decided to go virtual was so I could spend more time with them.

Family Life Is a Priority

I have a personal rule: I am home for either dinner or my children's bedtime. If I'm going to be late and may miss dinner, I make sure to be there for bedtime. If I prioritize dinner, then I return to the office afterward and miss bedtime. My family is my priority. It is important to me that my children grow up seeing that I was there for them, that I built a successful business to provide a good life, and that I actively participated in their lives. Sadly, I observed many entrepreneurs who, in their pursuit of business success, end up divorced or disconnected from their families because they prioritize money above everything else.

The Work–Life Balance

Now, money is undoubtedly important. It covers the roof over my head, the electricity in my house, the cars that I drive, the food on our table, and the clothes we wear. It allows me to spend time with my family. So, when it comes to work-life balance, it really all depends on what you feel and want to achieve. To me, balance is the key to success. I work diligently when I'm at the office, but once I'm home, I'm a family man.

Having a well-structured to-do list, or as I like to call it, "the get shit done list," helps me stay focused. Knowing what needs to be accomplished during the day allows for better concentration. However, emergencies are going to pop up, especially in software development. You're going to get a bug, you're going to get something that's just not working right, and you need to fix it and fix it *immediately*. Bugs and issues that require immediate fixing can throw your whole day off. Nonetheless, building a competent team is crucial. When you have a team that understands their responsibilities and can address issues promptly, it alleviates some of the stress. Of course, being an entrepreneur and a new business owner always carries a certain level of stress but having the right team around you who knows what needs to be done can reduce that burden and take some stress off.

To Sum Things Up

Believing in your idea despite criticism is crucial; after all, successful businesses often start small. Premier Virtual serves as a prime example of an idea born out of necessity, as traditional job fairs faced a decline. However, maintaining a healthy work-life balance is essential for entrepreneurs, necessitating the prioritization of family and being present in their lives. While money holds its significance, striking a balance between financial success and personal well-being is the key to long-term success. To navigate the challenges that come with entrepreneurship, utilizing a structured to-do list and assembling a competent team are invaluable. Ultimately, the path of entrepreneurship calls for unwavering belief, a strong support system, and a harmonious equilibrium in all aspects of life.

1. **Embrace criticism**: Every good idea faces criticism, but it's important to believe in your idea and its potential, even when others doubt it. Many successful businesses, including giants like Amazon, Google, Facebook, and Uber, started as small startups with a unique idea that gained traction.

2. **Believe in your vision and its potential to make a difference**. Even if you're entering an existing market, focus on improving and adding your own unique touch. Despite the challenges and setbacks, maintain a strong belief in your idea and your ability to make it a reality. Trust your instincts and persevere through obstacles.

3. **Adapt to market changes**: Recognize when the market is shifting and be willing to pivot and explore new opportunities. The birth of Premier Virtual came from adapting to the decline of traditional job fairs.

4. **Continuous learning and improvement**: Reflect on experiences, learn from mistakes, and constantly seek ways to improve yourself, your business, and your approach to entrepreneurship.

5. **Prioritize work–life balance**: As an entrepreneur, work-life balance is subjective and depends on personal goals and priorities. Prioritize spending time with your family and maintaining a healthy work-life balance. Strive to be present for important moments and avoid sacrificing personal relationships for business success.

6. **Money and balance**: Money is important, but it should not overshadow the importance of maintaining balance in your life. Strive for financial success while ensuring that other aspects of your life, such as family and personal well-being, are not neglected.

7. **Building a competent team**: Surround yourself with a competent and reliable team who can share the workload, address challenges promptly, and support your vision.

3

The Backstory

How does a small-town kid with little interest in school rise to become the CEO of an award-winning tech startup, creating a platform used by millions around the globe?

From Small Town to Soaring Heights

Growing up in the small town of Chippewa Falls, Wisconsin, life was far from glamorous. I often joke that my parents brought me into this world and then found their soulmates. With divorced parents and stepparents in the mix, it was an unconventional upbringing, but each member of my blended family imparted valuable life lessons. My mom taught me to work hard and go after my dreams. She always said I had a champagne taste on a water budget, because I always like the nicer things in life.

My parents and stepparents were pivotal in molding my character, instilling the virtues of perseverance and tackling challenges directly. Whether through serene fishing and hunting trips or the everyday hustle, I found comfort and motivation. These experiences taught me that real strength is born from confronting life's hurdles. Life wasn't always smooth, and there were times I fell short as a son, but the lessons learned from all my parents were invaluable. Even today, I apply these teachings, both harsh and kind, in raising my own children. At the age of 13, my neighbors became like a second family to me. They introduced me to jet skiing, motorcycling, and the art of responsibility. Despite moving away after just a year, they maintained contact, affectionately considering me the child they never had. The life skills they imparted continue to serve me well.

Sports became my outlet for joy, even though I was never the best at them. Boxing, baseball, and wrestling filled my days, and I managed to win the Wisconsin State Boxing Championship in the novice division—a small taste of victory at 15 years old. But as a small-town kid with average talents, I couldn't help but wonder if I could ever achieve something truly extraordinary.

Jumping Out of Airplanes

High school came and went, and the prospect of college seemed out of reach. Financial constraints and a lack of interest pushed me to consider a different path—the military. The call of the 82nd Airborne Division, with its daring parachute jumps and undeniable sense of adventure, intrigued me. So, fresh out of high school, armed with determination and a thirst for something greater, I found myself in basic training at Fort Leonard in Missouri.

Surviving the grueling challenges of basic training was only the beginning. My next stop was airborne school at Fort Benning, Georgia. Standing in the doorway of a massive C-130 aircraft, fear of heights threatened to hold me back. But I couldn't let fear define me. Gathering my courage, I admitted to the jump master that I was scared. He offered a simple piece of advice—to look at the ground and tell it that I wasn't scared. With trembling resolve, I managed to utter those words. And at that moment, as the green light flashed and the command "Green light, go, go, go!" echoed through the aircraft, I stepped out into the unknown.

Counting to four, my parachute opened, and I gracefully descended to the ground. Adrenaline coursed through my veins, and a surge of courage and determination washed over me. I realized that acknowledging and facing my fears head-on was the first step toward conquering them. The exhilaration and freedom I felt during that parachute jump were unlike anything I had ever experienced. In that moment, I shed the limitations of a small-town kid and became a part of something bigger—a brotherhood of warriors who faced their fears and challenged themselves to soar to new heights.

Following airborne school, I trained to become a parachute rigger at Fort Lee, Virginia. Stationed at Fort Bragg, North Carolina, the home of the 82nd Airborne Division, I embraced my role in the parachute packing division. Packing twenty-five parachutes a day became my daily task, pushing me to work faster and more efficiently. The meticulousness and attention to detail required in my work left an indelible mark on my character, fostering a keen eye for precision that would serve me well in my future pursuits. This is where I encountered Sgt. Meade, who profoundly influenced my life. He was a tough, no-nonsense leader of my squad. For even minor errors, he assigned me pushups. He also had me run around the Pack Shed with 20lb weights in each hand, simulating an airplane. While I initially believed he was pushing me away, he was actually strengthening me. My daily goal was to pack twenty-five parachutes; the faster I completed this, the sooner I could go home. Eager to avoid staying late, I quickly learned from my mistakes to minimize the pushups. Imagine holding a pushup midway, one dog tag perfectly flat, the other unmoved, for a full minute. It was grueling, but as my triceps and chest ached with pain, my resolve to improve only intensified. Eventually, I became one of the best in the Division.

But life in the military wasn't just about work. The camaraderie and sense of purpose within the 82nd Airborne Division were unparalleled. It was a brotherhood, united by a shared mission and unwavering dedication. We faced challenges together, supported one another through the toughest of times, and celebrated victories as a cohesive unit. The discipline and values instilled in me during my time in the army would shape my future in ways I couldn't yet imagine.

Little did I know that these early experiences—overcoming fears, working hard, embracing camaraderie, and cherishing the lessons imparted by my unconventional upbringing—would serve as the bedrock for my journey ahead. The small-town kid with average talents was about to embark on a path that would lead him to the forefront of the tech industry, defying expectations and creating a platform that would impact lives around the world. But that story is yet to unfold...

Sales and Making Other People Rich

I earned my sociology degree from FAU. I have a genuine passion for studying people. Given this interest, I always knew that my career would involve sales. After completing college, I entered the mortgage industry and was later recruited by a company that focused on outside sales. In that role, I constantly traveled, living out of suitcases and hotel rooms. It was during this period, before I had a wife and children, that I built sales teams for prominent Fortune 100 clients.

Our sales operations covered various avenues, including business-to-business, door-to-door, and retail sales. As the director of sales for the business-to-business team, I managed markets in New York, New Jersey, Texas, and Florida. I would establish a sales team in a specific market and then travel to different locations. Our approach to building sales teams involved utilizing job boards and attending job fairs. I made sure to attend every job fair available and ensured our presence on all job boards. It was during this time that I came across Career Showcase, a unique in-person job fair company that operated with exceptional efficiency compared to others.

After four years of dedicating myself to this company and enduring the grind of constant travel, spending nights in one city, then the next, and then yet another, I received a call informing me that my division was being shut down. They offered me the opportunity to transition to either their door-to-door sales division or their retail sales division, but I declined their offer. Instead, I accepted the modest severance package they provided and vowed never to work for corporate America again, making someone else wealthy while having others dictate when I should stop.

Motivated by this experience, I reached out to Career Showcase and proposed an offer to them.

Job Fairs

When I contacted the owner of that Career Showcase, we had an extensive discussion regarding the available options. Option 1 was for me to work for him directly, option 2 involved hiring him as a consultant while starting my own job fair company, and option 3 entailed purchasing a license agreement to operate under his business model and paying him a royalty. Excited about the idea, I shared it with one of my closest friends from college, Gary. When I explained the concept of starting a job fair company to him, he asked if it was similar to college job fairs. I clarified that we would be redefining job fairs and making improvements. Over the next few weeks, Gary and I traveled around, attending different job fairs and analyzing their success rates. We carefully examined which ones were effective and which ones were not.

After evaluating the information gathered, I presented our plan and proposed strategy. We returned to Brad, the owner of the company in New Jersey, expressing our interest in purchasing a license agreement. Since Brad's company operated solely in the Northeast, we aimed to expand the license to include North Carolina, down to Florida, as well as Texas and Arizona. Brad, understandably attached to his company, hesitated to bring someone else on board. It took more than six months of negotiations to reach an agreement that satisfied all parties. Finally, in June 2012, Gary and I organized our first in-person job fair in Fort Lauderdale, FL, which turned out to be a tremendous success, exceeding our initial expectations.

So, what set our job fairs apart from others and made them so successful? South Florida had an intensely competitive job fair market, with instances of three job fairs taking place in the same city on some days, and even two in the same hotel at times. What made us different was our decision to hold our events in the evening, allowing people to attend after work. We recognized that job seekers weren't solely unemployed but often underemployed, making it challenging for them to attend daytime job fairs. This unique timing made us one of the two available options for them. Additionally, we introduced a different approach to our events called the presentation format. We gathered all the job seekers in one room where I provided guidance on resumes, appropriate attire, goal setting, and other essential information for their job search. Following that, company representatives would enter the room and present their organizations, introducing themselves, and discussing their activities, available positions, and reasons why job seekers should consider working for them. This format ensured that candidates in the room would only engage with the right companies, eliminating any wasted time and making the process highly efficient. We advertised our events based on the specific types of positions the companies were hiring for. Consequently, if a candidate attended, they knew it was because the organizations had a genuine need for their skills. Our events lasted two hours, and we remained busy from start to finish, offering an effective and efficient experience. I carry this approach with me to this day as I build Premier Virtual.

In 2017, we started witnessing a significant decline in job fair attendance, which was a widespread trend across the industry. People had shifted toward applying online, finding it much more convenient than waiting in line at job fairs. By 2018, the situation worsened. At that point in my life, I had been married for a couple of years, had two young boys, and the diminishing income was taking its toll on us. One day, Paul, a business coach, informed me about a company specializing in virtual reality. He suggested that we connect and explore any potential synergies between our ventures.

Like I talked about previously, I scheduled a call with the organization, and during the conversation, he introduced me to the concept of virtual job fairs. Until then, I had never heard of such an idea, but it intrigued me. The thought of being able to host job fairs without traveling to different cities simultaneously crossed my mind. At that time, my schedule involved driving to various cities for job fairs, such as Jacksonville on Tuesday, Orlando on Wednesday, Tampa on Thursday, with a late-night return home and exhaustion the following day. Being away for four days also meant I couldn't focus on selling in the office for the following month. The virtual option allowed me to organize events in those three cities, as well as smaller locations like Sarasota, Bradenton, and Ft. Myers, all in a single day, eliminating the need for travel. Once I witnessed the virtual job fair demo, I was instantly sold on the idea and convinced that this would revolutionize the way job fairs were conducted.

I came to realize that the person who introduced me to the virtual job fair concept had merely shown me a tool that was available. We organized a few virtual job fairs and quickly realized that we could create a better platform ourselves. Brad, however, was not a fan of virtual job fairs and wanted to continue with his in-person company. As a result, we mutually decided to part ways. Gary and I embarked on our journey to establish Premier Virtual.

Our belief was that millennials and Generation Z preferred applying online rather than waiting in line. We saw virtual job fairs as the future, although it required a shift in mindset. I conducted demos on all the active platforms at the time, bearing in mind that this was 2018 and virtual job fairs were still relatively new, not commonly used in the way I envisioned. I even encountered a few platforms that claimed I couldn't achieve what I desired. Nevertheless, I had a clear vision and sought a company that shared that vision.

Key Lessons from Chapter 3

1. **Accepting a Unique Upbringing**: Your unique upbringing and blended family provide important life lessons, such as the value of perseverance, pursuing aspirations, and working hard.

2. **Overcoming Fear and Challenges**: Joining the military and participating in parachute jumps provided the lesson of recognizing and confronting fears, fostering personal growth and the understanding that true strength comes from overcoming challenges.

3. **Unity and Camaraderie**: The military experience fostered a sense of unity and purpose within a cohesive unit, emphasizing the importance of cooperation, helping one another, and sharing in victories.

4. **Pursuing Personal Fulfillment**: The decision to choose a professional path that was in line one's genuine interests and passions, will allow individuals to make a positive influence on other's lives, in this case, by studying people and helping job seekers in their career journeys.

5. **Spotting Unique Solutions**: The job fair company's success was fueled by spotting novel elements, such as hosting nighttime activities for the employed and developing the presentation format to speed up the job-seeking process.

6. **Adapting to Change**: Accepting the notion of virtual job fairs after realizing the drop in job fair participation, displayed adaptability and a readiness to accept new ideas and technologies.

7. **Pursuing a Vision**: The decision to found Premier Virtual was motivated by a distinct vision for the future of job fairs and a faith in the capability of virtual platforms.

8. **Tenacity and Determination**: Tenacity and determination were shown throughout the voyage while negotiating agreements, looking for prospects, and creating a strong platform.

These crucial lessons have shaped the journey of a small-town boy, propelling him to become the CEO of a software business that has earned numerous accolades and built a globally used platform.

https://
Social Network
WWW
Hello
Support
https://
WEBSITE
Synergy
Branding
SOCIAL MEDIA
Investment
Creativity
Best Team
WWW
WEBSITE
Investment
Synergy
Communication
Jobs
Jobs
Thinking Outside The Box
Idea
12
Vision
Plans
sales growth
WWW
Communication
Synergy
Supply chain

4

Mentor Teams and Why They Are Important

To me, this chapter is the most crucial in the entire book. I owe my current success to the invaluable help and guidance from my mentors. They broadened my perspective, introducing me to ideas I had never considered and steering me toward greater success. Particularly, Shana, Bob, Roger, Terry, and Kevin not only mentored me but also held me accountable for my actions.

The journey of starting and running a business can be emotionally challenging. Mentors can provide emotional support, encouragement, and perspective during tough times. There are many mentor programs out there and most of them are one-on-one mentorships. This may work well for certain things, but I believe the team approach is better. I mentor several people but I am not an expert on everything and have one point of view. This is why having a team of mentors is crucial for the success of a startup. There are distinct advantages to having a mentorship team compared to just one mentor.

A business mentor team, often referred to as a mentorship or advisory board, is a group of experienced individuals who provide guidance, support, and advice to a business owner or entrepreneur. This team typically consists of mentors with diverse skills, backgrounds, and expertise relevant to the specific needs and goals of the business. The primary purpose of a business mentor team is to assist the business owner in making informed decisions, solving problems, and achieving long-term success.

Here are some key reasons why a business mentor team is important:

Expertise and Knowledge: A mentor team brings a wealth of knowledge and expertise in various aspects of business, including finance, marketing, operations, strategy, and industry-specific insights. This collective wisdom can help the business owner avoid common pitfalls and make well-informed decisions.

Objective Perspective: Mentor team members offer an external, objective viewpoint. They can provide feedback and insights that the business owner may not see due to their close involvement in day-to-day operations.

Networking Opportunities: Business mentors often have extensive networks of contacts and can introduce the business owner to potential partners, customers, investors, or other valuable connections.

Accountability: A mentor team can hold the business owner accountable for their goals and actions. Regular meetings and discussions with mentors help ensure that the business stays on track and meets its objectives.

Guidance in Problem-Solving: When faced with challenges or obstacles, a mentor team can help brainstorm solutions and provide guidance on how to overcome these issues effectively.

Personal Growth: Beyond business advice, mentors can assist in the personal and professional development of the business owner. They can provide coaching on leadership, communication, and decision-making skills.

Risk Mitigation: Having experienced mentors can help reduce the risk associated with business decisions. Mentors can provide valuable insights on potential risks and how to mitigate them.

Long-Term Success: A mentor team can help the business owner plan for the long-term success and sustainability of the business. They can offer strategic guidance and help with succession planning.

Continuous Learning: A mentor team encourages continuous learning and improvement. They can recommend books, courses, and resources to help the business owner stay updated and competitive in their industry.

Confidence and Support: Knowing that experienced mentors have their back can boost the business owner's confidence and provide emotional support during challenging times.

In summary, a business mentor team is important because it brings together a group of experienced individuals who can provide guidance, expertise, and support to help a business owner navigate the complexities of entrepreneurship, make better decisions, and ultimately increase the chances of long-term success.

A team of mentors brings diverse perspectives and expertise. Different mentors can provide insights from various industries, functions, and experiences, offering a more well-rounded view of challenges and opportunities. This diversity ensures that the startup receives a broad range of perspectives, insights, and advice. If you only have one mentor, you will limit the exposure to different viewpoints, strategies, and experience. Different mentors can help in developing different skills. For instance, one mentor might focus on leadership and team management, while another might provide technical or industry-specific guidance.

Startups face multifaceted challenges that span areas like finance, marketing, product development, and operations. Having a team of mentors with expertise in different domains ensures that the startup receives comprehensive guidance. With only one mentor, you may get a mentor that excels in one area but no other areas. More mentors equals opportunity for more targeted expertise.

Each mentor in the team likely has their own network of contacts and industry connections. This can open doors to partnerships, collaborations, and potential investors, expanding the startup's reach and opportunities. With the one-mentor system, you are limited to only one network.

Relying on a single mentor may expose the startup to a limited set of ideas and solutions. With a team of mentors, the startup can benefit from collective wisdom, reducing the risk of making critical mistakes. The combined experience of the mentors helps in identifying and mitigating potential pitfalls.

In the Startup world, things are always changing and what you need help with changes. With a team of mentors, you have the ability to roll with the changes while working with only one mentor, the ability for expertise and learning may be limited.

Mentors can hold founders and teams accountable for their goals and actions, ensuring that the startup stays on track and meets its milestones.

Having a team of mentors provides startups with a broader range of expertise, diverse perspectives, and a more comprehensive support system compared to relying on a single mentor. Mentorships, in general, are crucial for startups as they offer a wealth of knowledge, networking opportunities, and emotional support that can significantly contribute to the success of the business. The diverse expertise, networks, and perspectives that come with a mentorship team can significantly contribute to the success and sustainability of a startup. In some cases, a mentorship team might be more important than a board of advisers because of the direct, hands-on guidance and personal connections that mentors can provide. A well-assembled mentorship team can be a strategic advantage for startups navigating the complexities of the business landscape.

> *My dealings of Mentorship had four distinctive avenues. Each group had their own way of doing things and different types of mentors. I learned so much from each one, both good and bad. With all mentorship programs, the more you put in, the more you get out of it. I cannot say I was always the best mentee, but I do appreciate all the different mentors I had in this process. Below are the four different mentor groups I worked with and a little about them. If you are reading this book, you want to get better and should reach out to these or find a local mentor group to help you. There are a lot of one-on-one mentor options out there as well. These have benefits as well but I like groups so that you can get different opinions and view points. With a single mentor, you only get one way and what if they are not an expert in something you need help with.*

The company 1909 was my first trip down Mentor lane. They were running multiple incubators in Boynton, Delray, and West Palm. I lived in Boynton, so I joined that group. At the end of the incubator, they had a pitch competition. I won the Boynton competition, allowing me to proceed to the next round with the groups from the other cities. It was during this round that I met some of the people from West Palm and Delray. Their great ideas and successful businesses made me realize I should have been in those groups. These groups had companies a little more advanced than the group I was in. In the semi-final round, there were twenty companies pitching and they were only taking the top seven to the finals.

The final competition took place at an outside venue with a large audience. The judges were seated prominently in the front row. Each participant was allotted five minutes to go on stage and pitch their product or service, followed by a five-minute question and answer session. As the presentations unfolded, there were some great ones and some that had challenges. Pitch competitions are not for everyone.

Pitching your idea to over 100 people and judges grilling you on your business can be difficult for those that do not like being in front of people.

As the evening progressed, I found myself as the last person to pitch that night. After observing everyone read off their power points and struggle with the Q&A portion of the pitch, I stepped onto the stage. Unlike them, I never looked at my screen; I had everything memorized. I knew my business and my presentation. My pitch deck was flawless, my pitch was on point, and I was certain I won. Supporters were high-fiving me when I got off the stage, and even the other competitors said, 'no competition,' they knew the title was mine… Or so I thought.

Finally, as judges prepared to announce the winners, I positioned myself at the back, intending to step forward when they neared the announcement of the win-ner. The host called out, "In 3rd place Steve Edwards, with Premier Virtual." There wasn't a lot of clapping that happened, and even some boos. I looked over at my wife and I said, "I'm not going up there to get this award," I was pissed. There was no reason I should have lost. Many people around me also said that "You should have been in first place." My wife, Christine, told me to "Stop being a baby and go accept my award." And, as a good husband, I listened to my wife, and I walked up on stage and accepted the award, my smile barely masking my discontent.

My experience during that event taught me invaluable lessons. Not taking first that night taught me that it is not always the best pitch but was your idea relatable to the judges. That insight was very valuable. 1909 taught me so much about myself and how to improve.

Lessons from Pitch Competitions

Let's talk more about pitch competitions and the lessons I learned from this par-ticular one. My frustration stemmed from the discrepancy between my perfor-mance and the perceived winner—the consensus among the competitors was that I should have won that competition.

The next day, I reached out to the organizers of the pitch competition and asked to see the judge's scorecard. I didn't want to see the judge's names, but I wanted to understand their feedback. I wanted to learn how I could improve my perfor-mance and grow from this experience. I believe every failure is an opportunity to improve, and I wanted to see what they had to say.

One judge remarked that I couldn't even answer the questions about my business. Another comment stated that "this guy will **never get any clients,** it's not a great business." That's the kind of criticism that motivates individuals to prove themselves. I realized that sometimes it's not about how good you are, it's about who the judges are and what their passions are. Judges may look for something particular and if you do not mention that you can get docked points. There is no perfect pitch or perfect judge, you just must go up there and give it your all. I took that knowledge into my next round of pitch competitions, a topic we will get into a little bit later. Preparing for a pitch competition can be long and grueling, but if you do the right way you have a better chance.

During one of the *1909* weekly meetings, Terry was invited to talk about raising capital. At this point in my business, I thought I wanted to raise capital, so this opportunity was timely. We'll get into the do's and don'ts of raising capital in a later chapter, but at this point in time, I thought this was the way forward. I pulled Terry aside and told him that I really liked what he had to say, and I wanted to show him a little bit more about my business. He was helpful and receptive. As a result of this meeting, I was introduced to another mentor team, The Venture Mentoring Team.

The VMT, or Venture Mentoring Team, is an organization of successful business owners, individuals who have sold their businesses, and high-ranking corporate professionals. They generously volunteer their time to mentor startups. Shana, a member of 1909, afforded me the chance to pitch in front of the entire VMT at one of their monthly meetings, which hosted over 100 mentors. I received valuable advice from some of the mentors after my initial pitch. Following this, I was encouraged to submit an application to be a part of the VMT. I followed through with them and then I was granted a second pitch in front of the entire organization. This time, the mentors could see me, look at my application package, and determine whether they wanted me to join the VMT. This is one of the best decisions that I made, but also one of the hardest decisions.

Choosing the right mentor team holds significant importance as they can provide guidance based on their own experiences, steering you toward the right decisions. And what I loved about this organization was their commitment to investing time and effort in fostering growth, while maintaining strict guidelines against investing financially in the mentees. This clear distinction against investing financially in the mentees was solely focused on improvement rather than financial gain.

In the initial stages, during the pitch scrub, I faced considerable challenges, but looking back, I am grateful for the learning experience. I had four mentors that provided constructive feedback aimed at steering me in the right direction. Their guidance was not limited to pointing out my mistakes; rather, they provided alternative perspectives and approaches to consider. They were a constant support, always available to offer guidance and understanding. Even now, they still provide valuable support and insights. A good mentor just doesn't go away after six or eight or twelve weeks; they remain present. For example, I could text Roger in the middle of the night, and even if he may not answer me then, I'll get a call from him the next day. And the great thing about a mentoring team like that is if one mentor lacks expertise in a specific area, they can tap into the knowledge of another mentor within the organization who can provide the necessary support.

One night, I was at a pitch competition not as a participant but as an observer. They were charging a ridiculous amount of money to be a part of the pitch competition and I wanted to just go see it before I decided to put that money out. While I'm at this pitch competition, I encountered investors and individuals from all walks of life. Engaging in networking, I struck up a conversation with a particular individual. I told him that I was part of the VMT, and he looks me dead in the eye and said, "Yeah, there's got to be a place for everybody. Not everybody can get into my mentoring team and you're just not good enough." I thought to myself, "Wow this guy's definitely a ball of bright energy." I blew it off after that. I didn't even think about it. Now, let's fast-forward a little bit.

Navigating the World of Mentors

I got an email from the Veteran's program at FAU, informing me about a startup incubator they were hosting and inviting companies like mine to join the program. I decided to attend their information session and I talked to lot of other Veterans that were there. They pitched their ideas, explained the processes, and outlined their objectives. The best part was that it was free. Engaging with other veterans, conversing with them and learning more about their businesses was well worth it for me.

I have always believed the more you learn, the more you can earn. So, even though I was part of another mentoring group, I thought, why not get more mentoring? There may be something else that I could pick up to make my business better. This new group was a gathering of like-minded individuals, and we covered some topics that were familiar to me from my prior experiences. It was enjoyable to be around a group of individuals who shared a military background like me. However, our meetings were abruptly interrupted by the onset of COVID-19.

So, our in-person meetings transitioned to virtual. However, during this time, I found myself engaged in sales demos all day, which caused me to miss some of these virtual meetings. In retrospect, I can acknowledge that I didn't put enough time and effort into that Veterans group because of what was going on in the world at that time and the demands of my business. But, toward the end of this period, they said my favorite words: "There's a pitch competition."

I waited until the deadline to submit due to other responsibilities. So, on the last day, there were only a couple of hours left and I had to create an entire pitch for the competition. These pitch competitions often have specific requirements regarding the number of slides in the pitch deck and the allotted time for the presentation and subsequent questions. Consequently, for each of the seven different pitch competitions I participated in, I had to adjust my pitch deck to align with their unique guidelines and parameters.

The day of the pitch arrived, and we were presenting over Zoom, whereas the previous pitch competitions had been in person. This is the first competition over Zoom, and luckily, I got a little bit of energy in me and ended up winning that pitch competition. While it didn't offer any financial reward, it did pave the way for me to compete at the state level for Veterans Florida's pitch competition. The winner of this competition stood to receive US$3000 and some recognition. However, the other participants were veterans from some of the larger schools in Florida and they had some impressive businesses.

At the Veterans Florida pitch competition, it was another pitch over Zoom, and I honestly didn't think I gave a great pitch. I had to record it and submit it, and I'm not somebody who enjoys recording things over and over and over again to make them perfect. I gave one pitch and gave it my all and I sent it in. I didn't think that I performed very well.

The announcement of the state competition winner would be delayed for about a month, as they had the competition followed by their conference, where the winners would be revealed.

The conference finally arrived, and it was time for the winners to be announced. They announced the third-place winner, and I knew that person had given a good pitch. Then came the announcement for second place, and I knew that the company was solid and they gave an impressive pitch. I was a little surprised because I thought they were the ones who were going to win. However, to my surprise, they called my name for the first place. I was shocked and excited at the same time, not because I won the money, but because it was a validation of my idea and its potential.

To this day, I speak very highly of Doctor Kevin Cox and his mentoring of the Veterans Florida program at FAU. I frequently meet him at various conferences and networking events, and I actively encourage people to go through his program because I believe it's one of the best mentoring programs out there for veterans.

Now, because I won the pitch competition for Veterans Florida, and was the first one ever from FAU to win that competition, I got a call from FAU Tech Runway. They asked me if I wanted to join their mentoring program. I told him that I missed the deadline for the application, but they insisted on my participation, expressing their desire for me to be part of the program. I thought about it and asked myself whether I truly wanted to go through another program, especially after I've gone through three others. And, this program had some grueling requirements. However, maintaining my mindset of always trying to learn and get better, and not knowing who I can meet that can maybe change my life or change my business, I decided to move forward with it.

Again, I had to create some information and send it over to them. Afterward, all their mentors reviewed the material, and I had the opportunity to select my top choices. Simultaneously, they also made their top picks for all the companies that were going through this program. As a result, I was paired with a mentor team consisting of five individuals.

And do you want to know one of the mentors that I didn't want on my team? It was the same guy who previously told me I wasn't good enough to get into their mentor program! Interestingly, after completing the program, I made sure to remind him what he said. I reminded him that they came to me and invited me to be a part of their program, and I asked him if I was good enough now.

Sometimes, in life, there are moments when you say things you should and other times when you say things you shouldn't. However, I'm not somebody that's going to hold something in when somebody pisses me off. With this program, we had monthly meetings where we would go over my business performance, analyzed the numbers, and identified areas for improvement. Some of the mentors were very involved in the process.

Jackie from the SBA was amazing to work with and couldn't have been more helpful. But not all the mentors were equally beneficial. Some simply sat there on the monthly call and didn't have any input, valuable or otherwise. While the program itself was amazing and offered a lot of opportunities for my company, I learned something. I've discussed this with others who have gone through mentorship programs. Just because they're a 'mentor' doesn't mean they're better than you, it doesn't mean they're more successful than you or more intelligent than you. If they're not helping you to improve your business, they do not need to be on your mentor team.

Many mentees in these programs are scared to tell the truth to the heads of these programs. And in some respects, I found myself in a similar position at times. While I had phenomenal mentors on all my teams, there were also some individuals that we're using this mentoring to check a box, and I don't know what that box was. It seemed that they were there just to say they were volunteering their time, but they gave no real benefit to me or my business.

As we conclude this chapter, it's essential to address the importance of wading through the noise (BS) when it comes to selecting mentors. It's essential to ask them critical questions and seek genuine, insightful answers. Why have they chosen to become a mentor? What is their motivation for taking on this role? What specific aspects of your application caught their attention, leading them to believe they can assist and support you? Are they confident in their ability to offer sound advice? Can they draw from their past experiences to be effective mentors? But perhaps the most crucial question is: Have they personally experienced the challenges of starting a business from scratch, including the daunting task of investing their savings and retirement into their own idea? Understanding whether they have been in your shoes can significantly impact the relevance and value of the advice they provide. I am not saying that someone that only has corporate experience cannot be a good mentor, but if they have been in your shoes, it helps. I had one mentor tell me all the things I should do for marketing. They came from a 10M a year budget, I was bootstrapping, they didn't understand why I couldn't do what they did. That is the type of mentor that does not supply you with beneficial information.

Pitch Competition—SHRM Better Workplaces Challenge Cup 2021

In 2021, the Society of Human Resources Management launched a challenge. It was called a "Better Workplaces Challenge Cup" competition. This initiative aimed to seek out innovative workplace technologies that reinvent how the workplace is conducted. The contest aimed to bridge the gap between companies that are creating workplace technologies and their end users, primarily HR professionals and their workforces.

This was a global competition that had thousands of entrants across the globe. Applicants were required to submit a video showcasing their software or product along with their application to one of the major cities hosting the events. The top prize was US$50,000 plus investment opportunities. I submitted my application and was selected to compete in the Tampa region.

Out of the numerous entries, they narrowed it down to one-hundred and fifty companies throughout the country. Therefore, I considered myself fortunate that I made it to one of the one-hundred and fifty. But now I was going up against companies that had a more extensive track record in the HR space compared to mine.

During the southeast regional competition, I was competing against fifteen other companies. Recognizing that human resources encompasses much more than just talent acquisition and recruiting, I didn't have overly high expectations. My focus was only on a part of the broader HR landscape. Nonetheless, I thought it would be an excellent opportunity to get my name out there. Surprisingly, I was selected to participate in the southeast regionals in Tampa, and it got me excited, making me wonder if my idea had genuine potential. Before the finals, we received an email outlining the judging criteria, which I've listed below:

1. Will this business contribute to creating better workplaces where both employers and employees can thrive together?

2. Will this business provide value to SHRM members and their companies by helping HR professionals become more efficient and strategic?

3. Is this business viable and sustainable?

Knowing the judging criteria is crucial because it allows you to tailor your pitch strategically to maximize your score. While judging can be subjective, having an outline to follow provides some clarity. Heading into the southeast regional finals, I was aware that some of the competition had more substantial contributions to the HR community than my software did. Nonetheless, I remained optimistic and believed in our potential. During the live online pitch, I gave it my all, but unfortunately, I didn't emerge as the winner, and I didn't advance to the next stage. Despite not making it further, I was proud of myself for reaching a point I hadn't even thought was possible. The experience of making it to the southeast regionals filled me with excitement and a sense of achievement.

Through this experience, I realized that I should have included more aspects of HR in my pitch, showcasing a broader impact on the field. Perhaps that could have taken me further in the competition. Nevertheless, participating in the southeast regionals was a significant milestone for me. Making it to the second round and not winning didn't discourage me; instead, it ignited a stronger determination within me. It was evident that there were people who believed in me and the potential of my software, and that belief fueled my motivation to keep pushing forward.

1. **Accept Opportunities with Low Expectations**: The choice to join a startup incubator with low expectations and a little investment resulted in priceless relationships and experiences.

2. **The Value of Mentoring**: Mentorship is essential for both professional and personal growth. Your path can be considerably impacted by having mentors who are knowledgeable in the subject matter and genuinely interested in your success.

3. **Pitch Competitions and Learning from Failures**: Even if you don't win, competing in pitch competitions can be a worthwhile learning experience. Future pitches can be made better by reviewing criticism and comprehending the evaluation criteria.

4. **Selecting the Right Mentor Team**: The caliber of the mentors on a mentor team determines the effectiveness of the team. Find mentors who can offer insightful advice and who are aware of the difficulties you face specifically.

5. **Don't Let Rejection Discourage You**: You shouldn't let rejection from business or competition ventures stop you from pursuing your ambitions. Rather, use it as inspiration to strengthen and verify your ideas.

6. **Tailoring Pitches to Audience**: You can improve your chances of winning competitions by understanding the judging criteria and designing your pitch to appeal to the target audience.

7. **Continuous Learning and Networking**: Stress the value of networking and ongoing learning for corporate growth. Gaining good insights might come through participating in a variety of programs and getting feedback from diverse sources.

8. **Evaluating Mentor Contributions**: Determine whether mentors and mentoring programs are helpful in delivering beneficial assistance and pertinent knowledge.

9. **Perseverance and Belief in Your Idea**: Having faith in your concept and overcoming obstacles might result in unexpected achievements and advance your entrepreneurial endeavors.

5

A Word from Mentor Groups

Dr. Kevin C. Cox, Florida Atlantic University

I serve as the director for FAU's Adams Center for Entrepreneurship. I am also the director for FAU's Veterans Florida Entrepreneurship Program, and the lead instructor at FAU's Tech Runway New Venture Accelerator. My primary role is operating the Adams Center for Entrepreneurship. At the Adams Center, our primary focus is on providing best in class education to students, faculty, staff, and the broader community here in South Florida around topics associated with entrepreneurship and innovation. We certainly accomplish that by teaching the typical undergraduate entrepreneurship courses, and we have a series of more than five courses that make up that curriculum. Additionally, and perhaps more relevant and unique, is the Adams Center for Entrepreneurship's Entrepreneurship Boot Camp program and associated curriculum. I started this educational program just over 10 years ago, and since that time, it has been widely successful in terms of providing educational content to hundreds of founders. During the same period, the course has continued to evolve its comprehensiveness, level of sophistication, and impactful.

Most recently, I authored the new venture Launchpad 2.0 (second edition), the formal companion workbook for the program. The boot camp is unique in that it is not a for-credit course. It is after hours in the evening, and it is only 8 weeks (about 2 months). It is also explicitly and only practitioner focused. What we focus on is how to successfully approach, and do, entrepreneurship. In fact, it contains almost no history or underlying theory, instead, it is designed for entrepreneurs who are starting or will be starting or are thinking about starting a business. It includes all the elements of how to go from an idea to an actual business in a concise but also detailed, informative, and sequential process. Today, across all my roles, I have taught, mentored, met with, or worked with over 1,000 founders and startups.

I have also been a mentor at FAU's Tech Runway New Venture Accelerator since the program began, as well as having been the program's lead instructor. This has enabled me to witness firsthand the tremendous value associated with mentorship. It is particularly important for founders, and while it is educational, the mentor role is distinctive compared to the educational content I teach. One of the most fundamental and meaningful distinctions is that mentorship is explicitly personalized whereas typically education is not. The expertise, guidance, and insight provided throughout the process are tailored (or should be) specifically to the founder (or founding team) and their venture. Thus, it is not generalized, is it specific, and should be directly applicable to the venture, problem, challenge, or opportunity that the mentee is working through. Another unique and valuable aspect of mentorship is that while it is specific to the venture, the source is truly independent thereby providing both an outside and objective assessment of any situation—this perspective cannot be applied from someone within the team, and sometimes this perspective varies considerably from the founder's own which can be important. Having multiple mentors or a mentorship team exponentially compounds the value of the advice being both tailored and external/independent by allowing for, and creating, multiple perspective along with multiple experiences and diverse sources of domain knowledge.

To me, those two fundamental distinctions are both immensely important and simultaneously valuable attributes of founder mentorship. However, mentorship is important and provides value in a myriad different ways including but not limited to: access to valuable network connections and social capital possessed by mentors (e.g., customers, partners, vendors, service providers, etc.), avoiding critical mistakes (in some instances from knowledge gained from the mentor's own experiences), new ideas/creativity/problem-solving, enhanced reaction time, enhanced ability to identify opportunities (both more and faster), and reduction in uncertainty (and potentially risk) among many other valuable benefits.

Finally, there is one element that I find is often overlooked when it comes to mentorship and that is the socioemotional and psychological element and the associated valuable benefits this aspect of mentorship can yield. This is similar to the meaningful and essential bonds that founders should (often must) develop with one another. I always encourage any solo founders to start building out their team as soon as possible for this reason (among many other reasons). No one can achieve success alone—and even if someone could, it would not be any fun and would just make something that is already extremely difficult considerably more difficult. Not only does building a team result in the acquisition and vast expansion of resources and capabilities, this too provides psychological and emotional benefits when someone can share in the challenges, the wins, and even the losses. Similar relational benefits can develop with mentors. However, these are unique and distinctive from those associated with the team members because, again, mentors are completely independent/external. Yet, they are to some degree in the trenches with, or at a minimum cheering for and rooting on the founder(s) at every step along the way. Mentors should also have, or be developing, a deep understanding of every aspect of the venture and then do, to some extent, share in the wins and losses, though indirectly of course. These relationships can be genuinely important and valuable for any founder for a wide array a reasons as summarized here.

It is worth noting that while the preceding discussion is in some part based on my own observations and anecdotal experiences and knowledge. Every single one of the aforementioned benefits are widely and consistently verified and supported within the empirical scientific literature on the topic. Given the style and purpose of this book, I decided to spare the readers dozens of citations and lengthy reference list. But, as a research scientist myself, it seems appropriate to point out that value of mentorship is overwhelmingly supported by scientific literature on the topic.

Shana Ostrovitz—1909

My name is Shana Ostrovitz and I'm Executive Director of 1909. 1909, named after the founding year of our County, is a nonprofit organization dedicated to the holistic growth of entrepreneurs who give a damn about building a better tomorrow.

We're an unconventional business organization that recognizes and embraces various forms of wealth, including health, relationships, time, and values.

1909 is committed to providing entrepreneurs the resources they need to succeed. We offer our members access to a unique community, affordable workspace, business education programs, and mentorship.

I think I first understood the value of mentorship in an experience where I didn't have any. This was during my first startup. It's not that I didn't have supportive people in my life, but I didn't really have anyone in my life who understood what I was trying to do as it connected to my values as a human being. There was no one in my corner asking me the important questions about my why and helping me build something that matched that. Unfortunately, I found myself creating a business that wasn't aligned with my values or skill set, and instead was what the outside startup world was pushing at the time.

Creating a company is hard no matter what, but creating a company that is successful and sustainable over time is even harder. I believe that the clarity and vision you need as a founder is critical to building something that lasts, and having a good mentor can make all the difference.

As I've gone along in my career, and now help hundreds of other people in their entrepreneurial journey, it's become more clear that a good mentor will believe in you and your ideas and more importantly will stand with you through the journey of the ups and downs. Everyone wants to be connected to a great business that's doing well, but it's a special and important person who will stick with you when things are messy and hard. Moreover, mentors will never know everything or have experience in everything you're doing. If you're starting something new, it's likely you'll have to forge a path that no one has been on before. Therefore, mentors are not there to tell you what to do, they are there to provide guidance and insight in areas where they have expertise and to be a sounding board for ideas, challenges, and strategy.

I think the best mentors will focus more on the development of the mentee than on the development of the business. A great entrepreneur can create an amazing business, but an amazing business cannot happen without an entrepreneur who is focused and clear on their vision and has the support to continue down the not so linear path.

Scott Barlass

Before I get into why I believe mentoring is so important, I think you should know where I came from to talk about all this. I am a seasoned business veteran with management experience in large corporations and as a successful entrepreneur and investor. I led the development of over 600 new products when employed by Toro, Procter & Gamble, Newell, and Rubbermaid. My experience is managing various functional areas, including marketing, industrial design, sales, advertising, merchandising, graphic design, financial control, and engineering.

I am a co-founder of The Axiom Group which focuses on helping clients be more innovative through IdeaBase, a collaborative problem-solving software (ideabase.io) and the Prop Cognitive Problem-Solving Method. Our Client experience includes innovative companies, such as General Mills, Thomson Reuters, 3M, Mattel, Fisher Price, Verizon, Sherwin Williams, Michelin, Kraft, Cargill, Clorox, and Toro. The Industry experience includes Consumer Package Goods, Consumer Durables, Toys, Food, Energy, Medical, Dental, Software, and Finance.

I have mentored many men and women during my career and now spend a great deal of time mentoring entrepreneurs as a member of the board of directors for the mentoring program at FAU Tech Runway, and USA military veterans through the Florida Veteran Entrepreneurship program and launching the Christian Focused Business Mentoring Program for Journey Church.

Florida Atlantic University (FAU) serves more than 30,000 undergraduate and graduate students across six campuses located along the southeast Florida coast. FAU Tech Runway is an incubator and accelerator program and an integral part of the entrepreneurial ecosystem at FAU. Tech Runway supports about forty early-stage startups per year and provides them with the resources, mentorship, and guidance they need to succeed. It provides access to a supportive community of fellow entrepreneurs and resources such as workshops, networking events, and educational programs. This collaborative environment enables founders to learn from each other, share experiences, and build valuable connections within the local startup ecosystem.

My beliefs are that God's values of love, service, compassion, justice, and integrity are important in the business world and is working to build a venture mentoring program through Journey Church in Lake Worth Florida (gojourneychurch.com) to help business founders and leaders bring God's love and compassion to others through their business initiatives.

I see benefits for both mentors and mentees involved with a venture mentoring process. But the benefits are only realized when good mentoring is taking place. By good mentoring, I mean that the mentor's knowledge and experience matches the needs of the mentee (some of the needs may not be perceived by the mentee at certain times due to lack of experience), that the mentor and mentee have an ability to communicate openly and honestly, that the mentor is encouraging and has the mentee's best interest in mind and has nothing to personally gain nor has a conflict of interest, and that the mentor can dedicate enough time to address the needs of the mentee when needed.

Benefits for mentees include:

- **Experience and Guidance:** Mentoring provides entrepreneurs with access to experienced individuals who have been through similar challenges and have successfully navigated them or have learned from failures and disappointments.
- **Networking Opportunities**: Mentors usually have extensive networks within the industry or business community. These networks can open doors to potential customers, investors, partners, and other key stakeholders.
- **Accountability and Support:** Starting a new venture can be overwhelming and lonely at times. Mentors provide a support system and hold entrepreneurs accountable for their goals and actions. They can offer encouragement during challenging times, provide objective feedback, and help entrepreneurs stay focused and motivated.
- **Skill Development:** Mentors can help entrepreneurs identify their strengths and weaknesses and provide guidance on developing critical skills like leadership abilities, sales and marketing savvy, and understanding of operations and finances.
- **Expanded Perspectives:** Mentors can challenge entrepreneurs' assumptions, encourage them to think differently, and offer alternative viewpoints. This broader perspective can help entrepreneurs see new opportunities, identify potential risks, and make more informed decisions.
- **Emotional Support and Confidence Building:** The entrepreneurial journey can be draining, filled with ups and downs, self-doubt, and uncertainty. Mentors can provide emotional support, offering reassurance and motivation, and help instill confidence so the mentee can overcome challenges and stay resilient.
- **Risk Mitigation:** A mentor can help entrepreneurs identify and navigate business startup risks.
- **Access to Industry Insights**: Mentors possess industry knowledge and insights that can be invaluable to entrepreneurs. They can share market trends, industry best practices, emerging technologies, and other relevant information that may be crucial to success.

Benefits to mentors include:

- **Satisfaction from Making a Difference:** Mentoring gives mentors the opportunity to have a positive impact on the lives of entrepreneurs, thus mentoring can be highly fulfilling and rewarding. Mentors often receive a sense of purpose and satisfaction from witnessing the growth and progress of their mentees.
- **Personal and Professional Growth:** Mentors can also learn and grow through mentoring by gaining fresh perspectives, insights into new industries or markets, and exposure to innovative ideas. Mentoring can sharpen their coaching and leadership skills, enhance their communication abilities, and expand their network.
- **Development of Leadership Skills:** Mentors guide, motivate, and inspire their mentees, and in doing so, they can improve their skills in mentoring, coaching, and providing constructive feedback. This can enhance mentors' own career prospects.
- **Networking Opportunities:** Mentoring often involves engaging with entrepreneurs, fellow mentors, and other professionals in the business community. This provides mentors with expanded networking opportunities, allowing them to connect with individuals they may not have encountered otherwise. These connections can lead to collaborations, partnerships, and new business ventures.
- **Exposure to Fresh Ideas and Innovation:** Entrepreneurs often bring fresh ideas, innovation, and a unique perspective to the table. Mentors could learn from their mentees regarding emerging trends, technologies, and market disruptions.
- **Legacy and Impact:** Mentoring allows individuals to leave a legacy. They have the opportunity to contribute to the growth and success of multiple ventures and entrepreneurs, creating a positive impact in the lives of mentees and perhaps the world.
- **Personal Reflection and Learning:** Mentoring provides mentors with an opportunity for reflection and self-assessment. Mentors often find themselves reevaluating their own approaches, strategies, and decisions.
- **Recognition and Reputation Building:** Mentoring can enhance mentors' professional reputation and credibility. This recognition can lead to visibility, speaking opportunities, and invitations to participate in industry events, further strengthening their professional standing.

Keith Chaney—Peadbo

I'm Keith Chaney, Co-Founder and CEO of the software company Peadbo (short for Personal Advisory Boards). I was blessed with an amazing family, one that would do anything to help me reach my dreams in life. Unfortunately, nobody in my family had gone on to go to college. Nobody in my family had received an MBA. Nobody in my family worked for Google, McKinsey, or any of the other places I found myself during my career. So despite their best efforts (and their efforts were and continue to be amazing), they couldn't equip me with some of the tools necessary to succeed in these new, unfamiliar places.

This, paired with a foolish "do it myself" mindset, led to me bumping my head more times than I would've liked to during my career. Even when I was the hardest working person in the room, I found myself constantly being passed over for great opportunities to ascend professionally. Not because I wasn't qualified or didn't have the experience, often it was because I didn't have the right network to help me succeed. I learned the hard way that you can't outwork relationships, and only once I tapped into my network of supporters was I able to hit my stride and perform at my true potential.

Based on this experience, I decided to build a tool to help rising professionals build and manage their support systems in a way that makes it easier for individuals to help them on their journey. Everyone knows the importance of mentors, sponsors, and supporters—some even preach the value of building your very own personal board or mastermind group. The problem is nobody tells you HOW to do it. Simply put, every billion-dollar organization you can think of understands that it needs a board to help it reach its goals, and you should have one too. But it doesn't require a bunch of paperwork and legal jargon, you just need to ask a few people you respect, admire, and don't want to disappoint for a few hours a year (maybe a quarterly one-hour check-in dedicated to helping you reach your specific goals). You'll be surprised just how willing even your busiest colleagues are to help when given the chance.

I've had the privilege of serving on boards and establishing my own, and I can't definitively say which experience has been more fulfilling. The beauty of mentoring is that I often feel I gain more than I give to my mentees. This underscores the idea that giving is as rewarding, if not more so, than receiving. No matter where you are in your journey, I strongly encourage you to seek out mentors and offer mentorship to others, because the notion of being "self-made" is a myth.

Software Development and the Challenges

Choosing a Software Development Firm

Deciding on the team to build our software was one of the biggest challenges our company faced. Picture a scenario where you must engage in a critical conversation with someone speaking a completely foreign language, and you lack comprehension of that language. This analogy illustrates the level of difficulty we encountered during the decision-making process.

Looking back, I wish I had hired a Chief Technology Officer (CTO) or someone with a background in that industry. As nontechnical founders, we didn't even know what we were getting ourselves into. So, I did what every person would do, I looked to Google for the best software development companies. I organized numerous meetings and calls with potential developers Since we were bootstrapping the project and not backed by investors, outsourcing was our path forward. After thorough research and evaluations, we eventually narrowed down our options to three different companies.

Company 1 had the advantage of being conveniently located near our office, just a short five-minute drive away. During our initial meeting, we engaged in a detailed discussion about our project's objectives, how we envisioned it, and the specific features we desired. However, when it came down to the financial aspect, they presented us with a price tag of US$250,000. Additionally, they required a substantial upfront payment. To top it off, they estimated a development timeline of over a year.

As someone with a background in sales, I couldn't help but question the timeline, thinking it shouldn't take that long to complete the project. I inquired further, and they patiently explained the complexities of the software development, clarifying that the US$250,000 quote was contingent on establishing a framework with no room for changes. Any alterations would incur additional costs. After careful consideration, we concluded that Company 1 wasn't the best fit for our organization. Their approach and pricing structure didn't align with our needs and expectations.

So, we turned to Company 2. This was a sizable software development firm with an annual revenue of around US$60 million. I'd encountered them at trade shows and had brief conversations with their team before. Our initial phone call with them was promising; they delved into the project's details, and it sounded quite impressive.

Subsequently, they arranged a meeting with one of their project managers and a sales representative. I found myself on a nearly hour-long Zoom call, where they delivered an extensive presentation and death by PowerPoint. This presentation was so far over my head, and I didn't understand 90% of what they were saying. They used jargon and technical terms that were entirely unfamiliar to me. Around the 45-minute mark, I had to interrupt and ask them to pause their explanations because I felt lost.

In retrospect, and I hate to say, but they may have been salivating at the thought that they could drive up a huge bill with my less than par knowledge base. However, they presented an appealing alternative: a monthly fee per developer. The project time frame would be based on how many developers that I chose to use on a monthly basis. With this option, our company could make it as fast as I want, or I could stretch it out if I wanted to keep my budget down a little bit. What sweetened the deal was the inclusion of a project manager and a sales manager with whom I could maintain regular communication. At this juncture, this option looks substantially better than the first option we had considered.

Now let me introduce you to Company 3, which was run by a husband-and-wife team based in South Florida. We scheduled a face-to-face meeting at their office in Boca Raton. During this meeting, they took the time to sit down with me and asked me a multitude of questions. They provided valuable insights based on their previous work, which I found quite impressive. To top it off, I discovered they had collaborated with some acquaintances of mine, which added to their credibility.

What really stood out to me was their communication style. They talked to me in a language I understood and didn't try to talk above my head using technical jargon.

They talked to me in plain terms, almost like salesperson talking to another salesperson. They were talking my language, and I was eating it up. I was thoroughly engaging in our conversation.

One noteworthy aspect of their approach was their timeline commitment. They informed me that in December, they wouldn't initiate discussions until March when they'd present the framework and plan for our system. At the time, I thought this was a great idea. However, as I later discovered, it wasn't entirely accurate. But this experience served as a valuable lesson that I didn't repeat when working on the second version of our software.

Their proposal involved sitting down with me to capture all my ideas and requirements. They promised to have their developers craft a virtual platform that would be better than anything available on the market. Their pricing model resembled that of Company 2, with fees based on the number of developers involved, offering flexibility to adjust the team size as needed.

After much discussion, Gary and I decided that Company 3 was the right fit for us. They seemed to have the most in common with us and spoke our language, making us confident in our choice.

Development Firm #1

We had reached a point where we were eager to move our idea into the next phase of development. It felt like this would be the fun and straightforward part, but reality had a different plan for us.

By March of 2019, we had the front end of the platform ready for review. However, when we took a closer look, it became evident that what we had wasn't quite what we had envisioned, even though it looked impressive. In just four months, we had invested a significant amount of money and time into something that didn't align with our vision. This experience served as my first lesson in the importance of being closely involved with every step of development.

At this point, I faced a crucial decision: whether to start from scratch or continue with what had been developed. I carefully considered the design and the time it would take to redo everything and ultimately decided to push forward with what we had, hoping to make necessary adjustments along the way.

Two months later, a potential client reached out to inquire about our platform. I had worked with them in the past and they know the direction I was taking our business. Even though we didn't have a website yet and were still in the software development phase, they began asking if our software could perform certain functions. In my eagerness to please, I confidently assured them that our software could meet their needs. This experience served as another valuable lesson, reminding me that software development isn't an overnight process, despite my initial optimism, which I humorously referred to as the "easy button." It's worth noting that my Director of IT is not a fan of that comment.

To my delight, the potential client was impressed with what they heard and expressed interest in having me present our software at their conference. They represented a substantial sales and marketing company with over 300 offices across the country, hiring over 10,000 people annually. This opportunity had the potential to propel us to new heights, but there was a catch—I needed a website to showcase our capabilities.

Now, the situation demanded a call to our development team. I told them, "Hey, I just pitched our product to a company, and I need you to incorporate this into the system within 30 days." This was one of our first change orders, and it struck me that if we had gone with the first company, this swift adjustment wouldn't have been possible, or it would have come at a significant cost. The owners of our current development team looked at me and said, "You are a typical salesperson," but they assured me they'd get the job done. This news excited me, even though we didn't have a complete software solution yet. However, I knew exactly what we were building.

Fast-forward to August of 2019, our software is live, and we were in the testing phase. However, we encountered a slew of challenges unlike anything I had seen before. Bugs seemed to lurk at every corner of our platform. While they were promptly addressed and fixed, it felt like we were applying a bandage to one wound, only for three more to appear.

During this time, I made a pivotal decision to alter our business model. Instead of hosting job fairs for clients nationwide, I wanted to create a Software as a Service platform and license our software to power virtual hiring events. This marked our second major change order, and its implications became clearer over time. Initially, I thought this shift would be relatively straightforward, given my limited knowledge in this area. But, once again, I was mistaken. Transitioning from hosting our own events to enabling others to host events triggered significant alterations in the backend of our system. The developers informed me that a lot of work was needed. Although I knew this change would entail additional expenses and time, I recognized it as a better long-term solution for both Gary and me, as well as for our business.

During this period, we started to see a little bit of a decline in the performance of our development company. Our requests and requirements were met with difficulty, and it became evident that they were struggling to comprehend and execute what we needed. Matters escalated to the point where the husband and I engaged in a lengthy, unproductive discussion that did not end well. I contemplated ending our business relationship with them.

However, the situation took a different turn when the wife reached out to smooth things over. She assured me that she would become my primary point of contact, as it seemed her husband was uncomfortable with being called out for the issues in their work. This experience taught me a valuable lesson: Developers can be sensitive when you tell them that their work isn't functioning as expected. I learned to approach such conversations with tact to avoid causing meltdowns.

While the change in contact helped for a while, we eventually realized that we had hit a roadblock with their software development capabilities. As we delved deeper into the technical aspects of backend development, it became apparent that they couldn't meet our growing needs. They excelled in front-end user experience (UX), but struggled with the intricacies of backend processes. It turned out that their expertise leaned more toward website development than software development. This realization led us to the decision to part ways and seek a more suitable partner.

Changing Development Firms Mid-project

I didn't want to start completely from scratch, but given my increased knowledge, I decided to explore other options. I interviewed a couple of other firms, and some of them quoted outrageously high prices. Considering this, I revisited the original companies we had considered.

I reached out to them and explained our current situation and needs. I simply needed them to step in, fix the existing bugs, and develop the new features we required. Company 1's response was less than ideal. They asserted that what we were asking for wasn't what we initially wanted, essentially implying that we got what we paid for. They were pretty arrogant, and their arrogance left us with no choice but to walk away.

We ultimately chose Company 2. Initially, they performed admirably, but we soon encountered a roadblock. It became evident that there was a language barrier within their development team. This hindered our ability to get things done as quickly as we'd hoped because they struggled to fully grasp our exact requirements.

In December of 2019, we went live and began conducting beta events with our clients. However, we encountered a persistent issue with our chat feature, and Company 2 couldn't seem to resolve it. What was perplexing was that every time they fixed one problem, it seemed to break something else. We couldn't discern if this was intentional, perhaps an attempt to retain us as long-term clients. To illustrate, it felt like taking your car to a mechanic for a faulty left blinker, and they fixed it, but suddenly your tailpipe stopped working. These two issues shouldn't have been related, but they somehow were, causing a chain reaction of problems. It was frustrating, and my attempts to communicate and find solutions were met with excuses.

 In a last-ditch effort, I even reached out to the owner of the software development firm. Keep in mind; this company was generating around US$60 million in annual revenue. However, the owner's response was shockingly arrogant. I approached him as a CEO to CEO, expressing my concerns and outlining the challenges we were facing and how they could be improved. His dismissive reply was essentially, "I don't care; you're just a small company." Long story short, we decided it was time to sever ties with that company.

This pissed me off. It struck me as highly unprofessional for an owner to treat a client in such a manner. Frustrated and seeking resolution, I decided to consult my attorney to explore our options. Justin, my attorney, provided some sobering advice. He told me, "Steve you could file a lawsuit against them, but you would be lawsuit number 93 in a long line of legal battles involving this company." He went on to explain that the owner of this company had a history of dragging out legal proceedings, knowing that many startup companies would eventually give up due to the costs and resources involved. His deep pockets allowed him to adopt this strategy with indifference.

This experience underscored an important life lesson and a crucial factor to consider when choosing companies to develop your software. It emphasized the need for thorough research into the companies you intend to engage with. If a company has a track record of being involved in ninety-two lawsuits, it's a clear sign that you might want to think twice about doing business with them.

At this stage, we had moved on to our third development firm. We were introduced to another local company that came in, addressed the existing bugs, but voiced concerns about the quality of the code, likening it to "spaghetti code," suggesting that it needed a complete overhaul. They were a pleasure to collaborate with, but unfortunately, they couldn't execute the project quickly enough to meet our urgent event deadline. Nevertheless, they continued working on other projects for us.

In search of a solution, I was directed to a fourth development team, known for their ability to swiftly rectify our chat-related issues and ensure smooth functionality within a week. It was widely believed that achieving such a turnaround was improbable. To our surprise, 2am.tech stepped in and played the hero. Their developer proved to be highly efficient and a pleasure to work with, ultimately rescuing us from the situation.

I then approached the owner of that company, expressing my admiration for the developer who had worked on our system. I proposed bringing him on board as a full-time team member, and we successfully hired him as a full-time developer. Subsequently, we also added another developer from 2am.tech, followed by a third. This approach proved to be more cost-effective, especially since I had come to the realization that we needed to undertake a substantial rebuild.

This was in early 2020, and I must admit I wasn't pleased with our progress. We found ourselves investing money into resolving bugs, and it struck us that it might make more financial sense to maintain the existing legacy system as it is, while simultaneously working on building a completely new, robust platform from scratch. I aspired to achieve the best possible outcome. We had already invested nearly US$200,000, and I believed we should be further along. Gary and I deliberated and devised a plan: Rather than merely addressing existing issues, we made the bold decision to build an entirely new software system from scratch. It was like tearing down a house to its foundation and reconstructing it from the ground up.

2am.tech played a pivotal role in this process. They not only rectified all the issues on our original legacy platform, stabilizing it and ensuring it worked smoothly, but they also initiated the development of version 2.0 of our platform. We expanded our team to include five developers from their team, and we embarked on a comprehensive rebuilding process. Additionally, we conducted focus groups with our clients to understand their preferences and gather insights on what they wanted to see in the platform.

As we entered March 2020, the world underwent a sudden and drastic transformation, shifting toward a virtual landscape. Premier Virtual appeared to be well-prepared for this new era—or so we believed.

1. **The Importance of Technical Expertise**: As a nontechnical founder, the author realized the importance of having technical expertise within their team, highlighting the need for a CTO or someone well-versed in software development when venturing into such projects.

2. **Thorough Research is Crucial**: The process of selecting a software development firm requires extensive research and evaluation. Rushing into decisions can lead to costly mistakes.

3. **Beware of Unrealistic Timelines:** Don't underestimate the time required for software development. Unrealistic expectations can lead to disappointment and frustration.

4. **Effective Communication Is Key**: Effective communication with developers is vital. Avoiding technical jargon and ensuring a shared understanding of project details can prevent misunderstandings.

5. **Flexible Pricing Mod**els: Consider flexible pricing models that align with your project's needs, such as monthly fees per developer, allowing you to scale your project as required.

6. **Be Engaged in the Development Process**: Stay closely involved in every stage of development to avoid surprises and setbacks. This level of engagement can help ensure the project aligns with your vision.

7. **Adaptability and Change**: Be open to adapting your business model when necessary. Recognize that changes may lead to additional costs and require more time but can yield better long-term solutions.

8. **Choosing the Right Development Team**: Selecting the right development team is critical. Ensure they understand your vision, speak your language, and have the technical expertise to execute your project effectively.

9. **The Value of a Diverse Mentor Network**: This chapter demonstrates the importance of having a diverse network of mentors who can provide guidance and support in navigating challenges related to software development and business decisions.

10. **Due Diligence in Legal Mat**ters: When considering legal action against a company, conduct thorough due diligence on their litigation history to avoid protracted legal battles.

11. **Resilience Amid Setbacks**: The author's journey illustrates the need for resilience when facing challenges and setbacks in the software development process. Staying committed to your goals is essential.

12. **Prepare for Rapid Changes**: Unexpected global events, like the shift to virtual environments in early 2020, can impact business plans. Being prepared to adapt quickly is crucial.

These key lessons stem from the author's experiences in selecting software development firms, managing project expectations, and navigating the challenges of software development and entrepreneurship.

7

Building a Team

Workplace Culture

Patricia Fripp said, "A team is not just people who work at the same time in the same place, a real team is a group of very different individuals who share a commitment to working together to achieve common goals." Many entrepreneurs face the question of when to expand, when to onboard initial or subsequent employees, and similar inquiries. Making that decision to hire is always a tough one because of the inherent question: Can the expert in the domain execute the task more effectively, or is the delegation of responsibilities necessary to take things off your plate? That was a very difficult decision for me.

As of January 2020, our team consisted of a mere four members. The onset of the COVID-19 pandemic, however, ushered in a transformative period. Suddenly, our phones were ringing increasingly, and the responsibility of conducting software demonstrations fell solely upon me. My routine shifted dramatically, with mornings starting as early as 6:00 AM and often concluding well past midnight—a testament to the unprecedented and unsettling nature of the pandemic's initial impact. Balancing these demanding hours with my responsibilities at home, where my wife and two young children awaited, became increasingly challenging. Regrettably, the extensive hours at the office meant limited quality time with my family—a situation that contradicted the family-oriented lifestyle I held dear. The disconnect between my personal values and the reality of my situation became evident, prompting a crucial realization: Change was imperative. It became clear that I could not sustain this pace; the sacrifices were compromising both my family's well-being and my own. This marked the turning point that underscored the necessity of expanding our team. This is when I knew I had to start hiring people.

"Steve," my friends reminded me, "you said you always wanted to change the world and that your software would do it. Now is the time," my friends said. These friends were individuals I had shared more than two decades of my life with. They, unfortunately, were affected by the economic upheaval caused by COVID-19, which prompted them to seek new avenues. Moved by their situation, I offered them a place in our venture. The result was a rapid expansion, propelling our modest team of four to a peak of twenty members.

Hiring Friends—Good or Bad

We grew fast. However, as we expanded, it became clear that speed wasn't always synonymous with success. Delegation became essential, and in the process, I encountered instances where my decisions fell short. Amidst these trials, there were commendable hires, individuals who enriched out team. However, there were also less fortunate choices, leading to suboptimal outcomes. The challenge lay not only in delegating but in selecting the right areas to entrust. Regrettably, I veered from my core strengths—the art of sales and nurturing client relationships. I got so focused on developing the best software that I took my eyes off what the prize was. There were instances when I found myself immersed in development discussions, sidelining the essential sales calls. In my conviction that I was heading in the right direction, I was blindsided by the realization that my energies were often misaligned.

With the company's growth trajectory, I took a significant step by bringing in a VP of Sales and Director of Sales. My intention was for them to spearhead the sales team while I focused on collaborating with our developers. Simultaneously, we were engrossed in developing the second version of our software. I believed my presence was pivotal and I thus committed to daily calls with the development team. Yet, my expectations fell short on the sales side of the house. The individuals I entrusted with leadership roles weren't the right fit, not due to a lack of effort but because their strengths didn't align with the positions.

I always adhered to the principle of hiring individuals based on their positive work ethic and a willingness to learn—a student mentality, if you will. My philosophy is anchored in the idea of hiring for attitude and then training for skills. My conviction was that if people could give me that positive work ethic and a student mentality, I could teach them the knowledge required for them to understand and effectively sell our product. But guess what? It's not just all about sales.

We had people in our team that had phenomenal attitudes, but they weren't in the right position. Recognizing this, we instigated changes, introducing new roles and rearranging responsibilities. Remarkably, these adjustments have borne fruit, with many of these individuals continuing to excel within our company to this day. Reflecting on this experience, several essential considerations emerged.

Firstly, evaluating individuals' demands poses fundamental questions: Are they loyal to the company's mission? Do they exhibit genuine dedication? Are they believers in our product and its potential impact? Moreover, do they resonate with the company's culture? These attributes form the bedrock upon which a company can thrive, making these qualities pivotal when building a team.

On the contrary, are there individuals who vehemently oppose any change or innovation? Do some individuals attempt to sow discord among partners and leadership? Do they prioritize their individual preferences over collaborative efforts? Evaluating these dynamics is equally critical. The broader employee experience is a telling indicator of a team's effectiveness.

Recognizing the significance of diversity, having people around you that have experience in other places that you don't is extremely important. Don't hire people the same as you. You need to be able to lean on people that know more in certain aspects than you do. Remember, it's a two-way street where individuals contribute unique insights and competencies that contribute to the collective growth.

What you don't want is people that fight every single aspect that you try to employ. Avoiding individuals who habitually resist change is paramount. Their presence can hinder progress and sow discord. In this context, the impact of a poor hiring decision is significant, with potential costs reaching substantial figures. No leader will ever make all the right decisions, but pivots and change are commonplace in the startup world.

Reflecting on this journey, the wisdom of John Maxwell resonates: The capacity to not only do great work for others yourself but to find others to help you do great work, where they have the same vision, and the same values can make 1 + 1 = 3, 4, or even 5.

When I was building a sales team early on in my career, I always said sales was the most important aspect of every business. I believed that for the longest time because sales brought in all of the money for the company. It was a simple equation: People wouldn't have jobs if we can't bring in sales and revenue.

However, the growth of my company brought about a transformative realization. Growing my company taught me that this viewpoint was the absolute wrong way to look at any business out there. Let's look at how business is like a big wheel. All pieces need to work together for an organization to run smoothly.

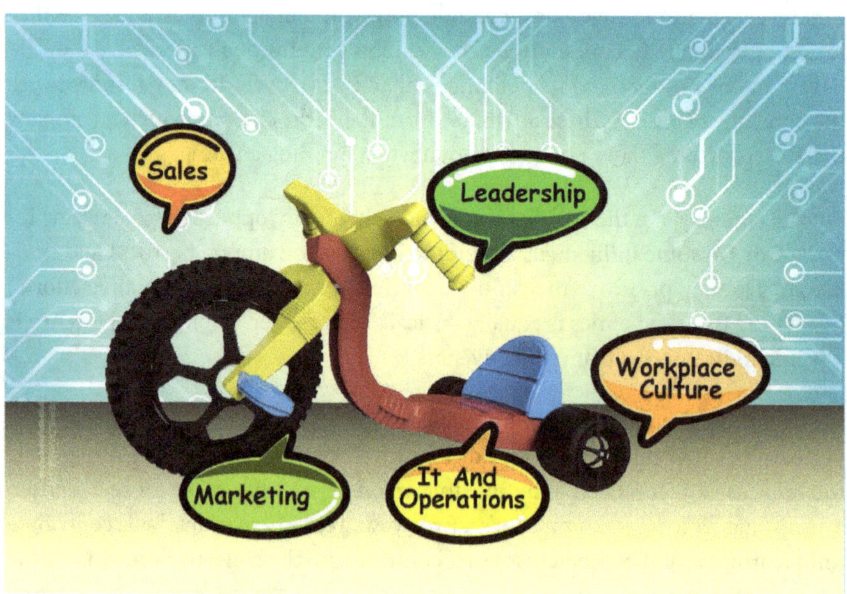

Big Wheel as a Business

Sales—That is the big wheel that keeps the company going and bringing in the revenue. You need sales to bring in the money and to bring in the clients. Just as the wheel's spokes extend outward, envision **Marketing** as the pedals. Marketing brands the company and impels the company's identity forward, ensuring its recognized and comprehended. The dynamic partnership between sales and marketing drives the momentum of the wheel; should this partnership falter, so does the wheel's movement.

Running parallel to the marketing pedals are the leadership team, functioning as the guiding handlebars. They steer the company's trajectory, aligning the strategic choices with the overarching vision. Their role transcends mere direction; they harmonize the collective efforts, ensuring the wheel stays its course.

The wheel's foundation, its base, encompasses **Operations**, **HR**, **Finance**, and **Support**—the support system. This is what holds the company together. To me, support is a very vital role within the company and normally does not get enough credit. Operations maintains the wheel's daily rotation, HR nurtures the team's growth, Finance allocates resources astutely, and Support bridges the company and its clients, fostering satisfaction and loyalty.

As the wheel completes its revolution, the seat symbolizes the **IT Department**, analogous to spokes connecting all segments. Their technical prowess transforms leadership's vision into reality, playing a pivotal role in innovation and delivery.

But no journey is whole without the back wheels—**Culture** and **Employee Experience**. Like the back wheels stabilize the entire structure, a healthy company culture maintains equilibrium and momentum. The alignment of attitudes, values, and interactions propels the wheel, underscoring the company's stability and longevity. Take away the company culture (back wheels) or have a toxic culture, the company can still move forward, but it will be at a slower pace.

In this broader perspective, it's clear that while sales remain a cornerstone, a sole focus on them overlooks the intricate interdependence of all elements. In the world of business, harmony prevails. Every facet is integral, and their symbiotic collaboration propels not only the wheel but the entire company forward.

Client Support and Client Success: Nurturing Relationships and Success

Within Premier Virtual, our support structure operates on two tiers. We have our **Customer Support** that handles basic day-to-day questions from clients, organizations, and attendees that use our platform. But then, we have a **Client Success Team**. This team is an integral part of our business model and the face of our company. Every client has a dedicated client success manager that walks them through training of the platform and is always available for any questions that they may have. This daily interaction sets us apart, ensuring our clients have access to assistance and scheduling flexibility. We prioritize their training to ensure seamless navigation of the system, accommodating software updates and organizational transitions. Furthermore, our clients enlighten us with novel applications of our software, creating a reciprocal learning environment. This team's dedication is instrumental in fostering client contentment.

OPERATION EXCELLENCE: ENSURING SMOOTH SAILING

The foundation of operation cohesion lies with Operations—the linchpin overseeing the seamless execution of daily activities. Ranging from payroll to benefits, this facet handles the vital components that maintain the company's rhythm. A standout among our team, Gary, our COO, does a phenomenal job at operations. He is often likened to a Swiss army knife because he's got his hands on everything and ensures everything functions harmoniously.

IT DEPARTMENT: THE ENGINE OF INNOVATION

Central to our technological prowess is the **IT Department**, the seat of innovation in a software company like ours. This team is responsible for translating leadership's vision into concrete technical developments. Bridging the divide between diverse perspectives—that of sales and developers—is an acquired art. Sales brains and developer brains see things in a different light.

An essential player in this endeavor is our **UX/UI Team**, a critical component that ensures our products align with user expectations. Our collaborative approach involves frequent discussions and weekly sprint calls, uniting leadership, operations, Client Success, and IT members. By fostering effective communication and understanding, we craft not only novel features, but also enhancements that address clients' challenges. The subsequent development phase involves translating these ideas into a language comprehensible to our software developers. This process culminates in the diligent scrutiny of a **Quality Assurance** Team that identify bugs and devise enhancements that refine our platform. In totality, this sequence of coordinated efforts takes place within the domain of IT.

CULTIVATING CULTURE AND EMPLOYEE EXPERIENCE: THE WHEELS OF PROGRESS

Lastly, the back wheels. This is your **Workplace Culture** and **Employee Experience** where the true essence of a thriving organization resides. This is what really makes the company roll along smoothly: it is the driving force that propels the company forward. I believe culture is probably one of the most important things out there—where team members are recognized as partners rather than mere employees, so much that my *TEDx talk* was on this exact message. The talk underscored the importance of recognizing team members as partners rather than mere employees.

Illustrating the practical implementation of this philosophy, **Premier Virtual** has been honored with consecutive recognitions as a top workplace by *Florida Trend Magazine* and the *South Florida Business Journal.* This recognition is unique, as it's our own team members who nominate the company. They contribute valuable insights through comprehensive surveys, delving into every minutia of their job and the organization environment.

Gary and I take immense pride in the fact that our team members genuinely love what they do and where they work. We are very proud that our team members feel this way. Not often do all your team members love where they are at. We don't look at them as employees, we look at them as partners and valued members of our team. Building an enriching culture has to be a team effort, transcending hierarchies. In this pursuit, soliciting input from team members provides a pulse of the organization's dynamics. Conducting individual monthly meetings with your team that veer away from work-related discussions gives them the reins to lead the conversation. This approach not only deepens their connection with the organization, but also positions leaders as mentors rather than mere supervisors. Taking these principles to the next level helps establishing a dedicated **Culture Team** within your organization to orchestrate events that resonate with the diverse spectrum of team members. This is more than an annual trip; it's a dynamic endeavor encompassing a wide range of backgrounds, positions, and ages. By planning monthly or bi-monthly events, this team crafts experiences that genuinely engage and inspire, fostering a culture that thrives beyond mere rhetoric. The ultimate goal is not just to speak about a great culture, but to tangibly build and sustain it.

If we examine the chart I introduced earlier, it's evident that every division within a company operates in concert, creating the cohesive entity that is the Premier

Virtual family. However, it's crucial to note that if any element of this interconnected system is removed, the entire company structure could be at risk of crumbling—except for the foundational back wheel. Removing these crucial components might lead to a compromised culture, resulting in slower and less seamless progress for the big wheel and the company as a whole. This underscores the paramount significance of company culture within an organization, illustrating why it holds such vital importance.

Key Lessons from Chapter 7

1. **Recognize the Need for Expansion**: When responsibilities become overwhelming, acknowledging the need to expand and hire is essential for sustained growth.

2. **Select the Right Team**: Prioritize team members aligned with your mission, dedicated to the product, and in harmony with the company culture.

3. **Delegate Effectively**: As the company grows, delegation becomes crucial. Entrust tasks to the right people for success.

4. **Stay Focused on Core Strengths**: Amid expansion, maintain focus on core strengths and avoid diverting attention from essential areas.

5. **Adapt Leadership Roles**: Flexibility in assigning roles based on strengths ensures the best fit for leadership positions.

6. **alue Attitude in Hiring**: A positive work ethic and willingness to learn often outweigh skills alone when hiring.

7. **Foster Business Harmony**: Successful business requires synergy across functions—sales, marketing, leadership, operations, HR, finance, support, IT, and culture.

8. **Prioritize Client Support and Success**: Dedicate resources to excellent support and a client success team for loyal customers.

9. **Excel in Operations**: Strong operational foundation ensures smooth execution of daily activities and rhythm.

10. **Nurture Innovation via IT**: IT drives innovation; effective collaboration between sales and development is crucial.

11. **Cultivate a Strong Culture**: Treat team members as partners, fostering a positive company culture.

12. **Engage Employees**: Regular communication, events, and mentorship strengthen connections and contribute to a thriving culture.

13. **Interconnected Ecosystem**: Every division plays a vital role; removal of any part, except culture, risks overall stability and progress.

To Raise Capital or Not?
A Decision for Entrepreneurs

To Raise Capital or Not: a Decision for Entrepreneurs

Every young entrepreneur with an idea eventually faces the question: to raise capital or not? In this chapter, I'll share my experiences dealing with Venture firms and Angel investors. While my book delves into the challenges of startups and the obstacles I encountered, those considering the VC route should also read *Venture Deals* by Brad Feld and Jason Mendelson. This book provides valuable insights into the world of VC funding, including its pros and cons.

As for me, I chose the bootstrap route, deeming it best for my business and myself. Do I sometimes wonder if seeking investors could have been a good choice? There have been moments when I thought that taking that path might have propelled me further. However, a mentor once told me every dollar you earn is a dollar you don't need to raise externally, implying fewer percentages given away. This advice deserves careful consideration when weighing the pros and the cons, especially if you have value maintaining total control, as bringing in investors might not align with that vision.

Choosing the Right Funding Path for Your Startup

Selecting the right funding path for a startup is a critical decision that significantly impacts its growth and future trajectory. The choice between bootstrapping, angel investors, or VC funding depends on various factors: including the startup's stage, growth potential, funding needs, and long-term goals. In the realm of finance and investment, VC firms, angel investors and private equity firms play vital roles in nurturing startup success. Although they all provide financial support, each entity functions uniquely, contributing to the entrepreneurial landscape in distinct ways.

Considering Your Options: Bootstrapping, Angel Investors, and VC Funding

Here are some considerations to help guide the decision-making process:

1. <u>Bootstrapping</u>:

Bootstrapping refers to self-funding or utilizing personal resources to initiate and grow a business. This approach allows founders to maintain complete control and ownership of their company but requires them to also bear the financial burden. Consider bootstrapping if:

- your funding needs are limited, and the startup can generate early revenue or attract customers without substantial external investment.
- your goal is to validate your business model and market demand before approaching investors.
- autonomy and control are priorities, and you wish to avoid diluting equity or involving external stakeholders.

2. <u>Angel Investors</u>:

Angel investors offer capital, expertise, and networks, particularly during the seed and early stages of a startup. They often provide mentorship and guidance, making them more accessible than VC firms. Consider angel investors if:

- your startup requires initial capital to develop products, build a team, or validate the market.
- you value industry expertise and connections, as angel investors bring valuable networks and insights.
- you need a swift investment decision, as angel investors can act faster than VC firms.

3. <u>VC</u>:

VC firms are well-suited for startups with high-growth potential and scalable business models. VC funding provides access to substantial capital and resources, it comes with higher expectations and potential dilution of ownership. Consider VC if:

- your startup operates in a high-growth industry and requires substantial capital infusion to scale quickly.
- you seek industry expertise, guidance, and strategic support from experienced investors.
- long-term exit strategies like IPOs or acquisitions align with your goals, as VC firms typically expect substantial returns with defined time frames.

Remember that startups can blend various funding sources based on their unique needs. For instance, a startup may begin with bootstrapping, then secure angel investments to fuel initial growth, and later seek VC funding to scale further.

Making and Informed Decisions: Research and Due Diligence

Ultimately, the best path is the one you understand the best. The choice between bootstrapping, angel investors, or VC funding should be based on a thorough assessment of the startup's financial requirements, growth potential, desired level of control, and alignment with long-term objectives. Research is key in this decision-making process, especially when navigating the complexities of funding options. Seeking advice from experienced entrepreneurs, mentors, or industry professionals can also provide valuable insights for making an informed decision. Don't rush into accepting funds; analyze all your available options.

Learning from Experience: Navigating VC and Angel Investments

One of the things that helped me make my decision on bootstrapping was this scenario I encountered. Let's walk through it: Imagine you have your startup, and you're faced with the choice of partnering with a VC firm or an angel investor. They offer a US$1,000,000 investment in exchange for a 20% ownership stake in your company. Initially that million-dollar injection might seem like a significant boost for your operations. Now, fast-forward to a point where you're considering selling your company for US$10 million.

Basic calculations might suggest that you'd receive US$8 million, and the VC firm would get US$2 million based on your initial ownership arrangement. However, the reality really isn't that straightforward. This is the juncture where delving into your contract details and having a proficient attorney becomes crucial. A lot of these VC firms will insert clauses into contract stipulating that they need to earn five times or more than their initial investment. But it's important to understand this multiplier and its implications.

Suppose this particular firm aimed for a 5X return. In that case, their take from the deal could be a minimum of US$5 million. As a result, this significantly alters the amount you might have anticipated receiving. Additionally, these contracts might involve various provisions that prioritize the investor's returns and encompass different types of stock arrangements. Numerous anecdotes circulate about startups where the VC ends up reaping substantial rewards while the entrepreneur or founder is left with little. It's advisable to reference the book mentioned earlier for a detailed explanation of these dynamics. Moreover, securing legal counsel can safeguard you from unfavorable agreements.

Venture capitalists and angel investors possess a multitude of motivations to invest in your venture, but it takes just one reason for them to decide against investing. Hence, being well-prepared is paramount. A robust pitch deck and a profound understanding of its content play a pivotal role when you're facing these potential investors.

Approaches differ: Some individuals opt to engage firms to circulate their pitch decks, while others directly distribute their presentations to various VC and angel investment entities. The logic is simple—the more eyes that peruse your deck, the higher the likelihood of securing an opportunity to present your concept. At this juncture, the topic of nondisclosure agreements (NDAs) often emerges. And it's worth noting that according to my mentor's insight, most VC firms won't entertain an NDA solely to review your pitch deck.

Navigating the VC Landscape: Lessons from the Trenches

Embarking on my first VC encounter unfolded like this: My connections led me to a local VC firm in Fort Lauderdale. Admittedly, I was too early for their typical investment stage, yet their willingness to engage stemmed from my connections. As I laid out my vision, the listener seemed intrigued. However, he outlined three prerequisites for serious consideration:

1. Construct a robust C-Level executive team.
2. Shift the business model from event-centric to an annual licensing structure.
3. Achieve US$1,000,000 in revenue.

Several months later, my experience led me to a pitch competition where I was asked to be the keynote speaker—an opportunity well-deserved, considering my previous wins in such competitions. While immersed in the pitches, a familiar face caught my attention: one of the judges was the same person I had engaged with at the VC firm. I promptly messaged him, highlighting that I had fulfilled all of his stipulations and inquired about revisiting our conversation. After a call, he expressed interest. However, subsequent weeks brought silence, prompting me to follow up. His response was unexpected: He had conversed with another similar company and declined interest due to market saturation. Here lay a revelation—investment decisions weren't solely about our performance, but about a host of factors. It dawned on me that each investor had a unique threshold for commitment, based on their specific criteria.

Another interaction with a different VC firm taught me another valuable lesson: Credentials on a business card don't necessarily correlate with expertise. Our conversation began with optimism as my CFO and I engaged with the firm's head. As we delved into our pitch deck, the conversation took a surprising turn. The firm's head claimed to have researched me extensively beforehand—an encouraging sign, I thought. However, it became evident that his "research" relied on hearsay from a friend within our industry. Unfortunately, this friend's expertise lay far from our realm. I stood my ground, conveying that the friend's insights were incongruent with our operations. Despite his persistence, I remained resolute in clarifying our business' essence. This experience solidified a key principle for me: Even in the face of apparent authority, it's essential to challenge misinformation or misunderstanding, as authenticity triumphs over arrogance.

The Angel Investor Experience: Lessons in Choice and Influence

Like VC firms, the realm of angel investors offers a mix of promising and less favorable options. Allow me to recount two instances where I engaged with angel investors. A South Florida-based angel investment firm with a solid reputation reached out to me, spurred by a pitch competition victory. They encouraged me to submit an application, a process requiring the meticulous assembly of a pitch deck and presentation. The proposal underwent group scrutiny, and if interest was piqued, an initial call with me and their team members followed—a chance to present in person and tackle an array of probing questions. These queries, intended to dissect my understanding of business, financials, and more, underscored why I value pitch competitions as preparatory grounds for facing the rigors of investor scrutiny.

Angel investors, typically affluent individuals pooling resources, unite to amplify their investment capabilities. Each angel investor has the opportunity to either say yes or no, and determine how much that they want to put into the collective pool. While US$100,000 investment may seem modest individually, a scenario where ten angel investors each contribute US$100,000, accumulates to a substantial US$1,000,000—potentially transformative for your business. My application was accepted, propelling me into what I fondly term "interrogation level one." Thoroughly responding to their inquiries propelled me to the second round of interrogation. This stage introduced more individuals keen on investment. This engagement was promising, fueling my enthusiasm for the organization.

At this juncture, our decision on whether to embrace the investor route remained uncertain. My approach was consistent across all investment firms: I sought not just capital but expertise. I yearned for a partnership where the investor would educate me, reveal uncharted territories and help navigate challenges. Although my business plan was robust, I acknowledged gaps in my knowledge. Surprisingly, my transparency resonated with many firms, highlighting the value of aligning financial inflow with mentorship and support. This underscored the wisdom in prioritizing compatibility and shared vision over mere funding.

Returning to the angel investment firm, I navigated through initial scrutiny, securing a positive response at both "interrogation" levels. The initial excitement was balanced by the waiting period—a monthly meeting where startups presented to the entire group, culminating in decisions on investment recipients. Following the meeting, a call arrived. The original contact echoed his enthusiasm for my idea and its potential. But the turning point—expressed a thorough "but." A senior angel investor, formerly running a recruitment firm, cast a shadow. His skepticism toward modern practices like virtual job fairs and video interviews led him to deem my concept unsound. His opinion swayed others, an eye-opening illustration that a single dissenting voice can tip the scales. This incident served as a reminder that unanimity is elusive and that the power of conviction can be formidable.

What I learned from that experience is that achieving universal satisfaction is unattainable. Not everyone will grasp your business, its model, or your software's essence. People get stuck in their ways and they get their mind set on one thing, and those are the people that you're just not going to be able to change. It's important to note that I hold no negative feelings toward that organization. Despite encountering some of its members on various occasions, I refrained from expressing any criticism. Instead, I chose to view this as a chance for personal growth, enabling me to discern what I aimed to avoid in my own approach.

My next angel investment group started the same way. They called me and I put in the application. The initial phase involved an interrogation round, during which they expressed strong interest in my proposal. The second round was a little bit different—all the angel investors convened for a Zoom call with me. This setup allowed me to observe their engagement levels: note-takers, inquisitive questioners, those seemingly disinterested, and those who kept their cameras off. This helped me distinguish genuine interest from lukewarm responses. The discussion became challenging as both my CFO and I fielded tough questions. We navigated through it successfully and progressed to a third level of assessment, yet another call that delved even deeper. As these calls get deeper and deeper in the process, they really are dissecting your business. They scrutinized its potential to yield profits, evaluating whether an investment could yield five to ten times return within a relatively short time frame. Engaging with these individuals requires understanding their perspectives and goals. This underscores the significance of the question I posed earlier: If you're going to invest in me and my company what do you bring to the table? Going through the Mentor programs prepared me for these types of calls.

If you're just saying I'm giving you money, it's not the right fit for me. For you that may be different. During our third in-depth discussion, we were poring over our financial records. At that moment, one of the participants raised a query about how we document revenue and handle commissions. Providing context, my CFO has extensive experience with multiple acquisitions, chosen for his expertise in raising capital and orchestrating business exits. As this participant began questioning, Bryan elucidated the principles of GAAP revenue and legal regulations. Despite this, she engaged in a dispute with him during the call, in the presence of all the other angel investors. Two significant outcomes unfolded: Bryan educated everyone about GAAP principles, and we realized that someone lacking comprehension of the financial dimension might not be a good fit for us. Despite the inclination to engage in the argument, we took the high road. After the call, I sent an email to the head of the group and included all the links for accounting principles. This gesture aimed to establish that our methods were correct and above board. Simultaneously, I expressed that this alignment wasn't suitable for us, and we would not pursue their investment and withdrawing our application.

The lesson I learned from this experience is that just because somebody has a little bit of money that they put away doesn't mean they're smarter than you, doesn't mean they're more educated than you, and it doesn't mean that they understand what is going on. It reinforces the importance of querying each potential angel investor about what they bring to your table. As you see, a reccurring theme emerges: The significance of posing questions rather than passively enduring their inquiries. What you are seeking is a partner who will collaborate with you, not just scrutinize your monthly figures to make judgments solely based on them. The real question is, can they help you grow and expand your business?

Another thing that we encountered where early-stage organizations expressed interest in acquiring us. I had multiple calls with companies that we're looking to acquire very early-stage startups. The typical pattern involved them approaching us, presenting themselves as either a small firm looking to add a few companies to their portfolio annually for long-term growth or as an entity intending to buy and uphold the legacy of our business. The arrangement often played out like this: They propose a buyout, offering a cash sum, which could either be substantial and immediately remove us from the business equation or sizable but tied to a commitment for me to stay on board for an addition two to three years while they drive further growth.

During my first encounter with this situation, a company approached me with an offer to purchase 75% of the business. They presented an appealing proposition of US$4 million in cash, with a requirement for me to remain involved for at least two more years. This proposal initially captivated me, as the notion of retiring within two years held significant allure. However, I countered their offer, expressing that the sum wasn't sufficient and stipulating that, if they were genuinely serious, the figure would need to be at least three times higher.

I had similar conversations with a couple of other organizations. These discussions revolved around valuation multiples of revenue that I deemed too low. Once again, I asserted my lack of interest unless the valuation multiple was substantially elevated. These sort of arrangements can be highly appealing for individuals seeking a quick financial gain. However, considering my responsibilities as a parent with young children, my retirement goals necessitated a larger financial cushion.

Lately, I've observed a growing trend in which individual investors express interest in complete takeover of companies. This involves assuming the role of CEO, assembling their own team, and running the business as if it were entirely their own. This trend typically initiates with communication vie email, LinkedIn messages, or phone calls. The message is clear: They are seeking a single company to take charge of, lead its growth, and essentially run the show. This approach has its appeal, particularly when they proposed taking over while providing a substantial exit fee and ongoing yearly compensation. It's an intriguing prospect—having someone step in, manage, and grow the business, all while ensuring a lucrative exit for you and consistent yearly income.

However, it's worth noting that these arrangements often involve a smaller upfront payment. While these investors may express their intention to maintain the company's operations over the long term, the underlying motivation might be to step in, drive growth, and then exit within a relatively short time frame of three to five years.

As you can see there are many options for you to look at and consider. You can also use more than one approach. Ultimately, the choice between bootstrapping, angel investors, or VC funding should be based on a thorough assessment of the startup's financial requirements, growth potential, desired level of control, and alignment with long-term objectives. Seeking advice from experienced entrepreneurs, mentors, or industry professionals can also provide valuable insights for making an informed decision.

1. **Strategic Funding Choice**: The decision between raising capital or not significantly shapes an entrepreneur's journey. Understanding the distinct realms of venture capital (VC) and angel investors is crucial. Balancing internal earnings with external investments can help preserve ownership and control.

2. **Funding Paths and Startup Growth**: Selecting the appropriate funding path for a startup hinges on its growth prospects, stage, and long-term goals. The choice between bootstrapping, angel investors, or VC funding requires careful assessment of financial needs and objectives.

3. **Informed Decision-Making**: Making well-informed choices is paramount in the funding process. Thorough research, due diligence, and seeking insights from experienced individuals can guide decisions aligned with the startup's trajectory.

4. **Navigating VC Funding Complexity**: Interactions with VC firms underscore the need for meticulous contract examination. Clauses stipulating return multipliers and equity distribution can significantly impact outcomes. Legal counsel is essential to ensure equitable agreements.

5. **Maximizing Angel Investments**: Engaging with angel investors highlights the value of transparency and compatible partnerships. Seeking investors who offer expertise and align with the startup's vision can yield more than just financial support.

6. **Early-Stage Acquisition Considerations**: Early-stage acquisition offers necessitate careful evaluation. Balancing immediate buyouts with continued involvement and compensation requires aligning terms with personal financial aspirations.

7. **Individual Investor Takeovers**: A growing trend involves individual investors assuming complete control of startups. Understanding the implications of these arrangements, including shorter-term focus and smaller upfront payments, is crucial.

8. **Diverse Funding Strategies**: Startups can blend funding sources, like bootstrapping, angel investments, and VC funding, to meet unique needs. Sequencing these sources can facilitate growth at various stages.

9

TEDx and Decision to Write a Book

TEDx

In 2022, I was invited to speak at a Future Influencers Seminar, which was the largest platform I had been offered at that point. The event boasted a lineup of highly accomplished speakers who were all extremely successful entrepreneurs. During this time, I frequently spoke at smaller sessions within conferences, usually these were mid-day sessions with around 100 attendees. However, I had yet to secure a keynote position. One of the fondest but particularly challenging speaking engagement was at the Florida Veterans Conference after Robert O'Neill, the SEAL that shot Bin Laden. Talk about a tough act to follow.

The day of the Future Influencer came, and I had to say, I was a little nervous. Not because I doubted my ability to deliver a great speech, but how would I compare to the other speakers. While I am pretty confident on stage, the other speakers boasted a long list of accolades. One had secured the Ernst and Young Entrepreneur of the Year award, another was a best-selling author, and yet another had authored multiple books and made appearances on several talk shows.

My chosen topic was, "The Future of Recruiting and Hiring," a topic I knew well. I had prepared an outline, preferring to speak extemporaneously rather than stick to a script. When I got on stage, I winged it. I knew what I wanted to say and made sure I hit my points. As the evening unfolded at Brand Start Studios in South Florida, I found myself in an unfamiliar setting—the venue was packed, and cameras were everywhere. While I recognized a few faces in the audience, I realized I didn't know the majority of the attendees. The speakers that came before me delivered awe-inspiring performances. Finally, it was my turn. Standing in the dressing room, I looked in the mirror and I said to myself, "You were born for this. You waited your whole life to be here and now it's your time to shine." I walked out on the stage and absolutely killed it. I hit every point I wanted and got a huge ovation at the end. I couldn't have been happier. This success marked the beginning of my pursuit of gracing the TEDx stage.

Shortly after the Future Influencer event, the applications were released for TEDx Boca Raton. I eagerly submitted my application video, highlighting how I started a business from an idea to execution in a short period of time. I just knew I was going to get picked, or so I thought. However, the call from the committee shattered my expectations—I hadn't been selected to speak. I was devastated and admittedly furious at this unexpected turn of events. But what made it worse discovering that several individuals chosen for the event were those I had shared the stage with at the "Future Influencer" event. I was just as good if not better than some of them. What did they have that I didn't have? It was during a conference in Dallas, while I was walking by the keynote speakers' area, that I had an epiphany. All the keynote speakers and the selected TEDx speakers all had something in common—they were all published authors. That was the missing link I needed. A light bulb went off in my mind, compelling me to embark on writing the very narrative you're currently reading. I knew if I took my stage presence, my story, and write a book, I would get on the TEDx stage.

Time to Write a Book

Deciding how to write a book is a story of its own. I considered hiring a ghost-writer. Every company I researched online said they were in Los Angeles and had authors in the United States. Which was false. I started one way but then pivoted, which is a trend I seem to follow. I start one way but then find a better way.

After discussing with several ghostwriting firms, I eventually chose the one I wanted. However, I found out pretty quickly why they were so affordable. They assigned a project manager that promised to oversee the entire process. During our call to discuss the book, we discussed that it would be about my story of starting a tech company. I sent over the book's outline. In response, they sent me over a cover that looked like a wedding book. Confused, I asked him if he read what I sent them and if he remembered our initial conversation. He said, "Yes, it's about weddings, right?" I instantly told him to have his manager call me, and I insisted that someone else manage my project. This incident was just one of many red flags that were adding up. Despite assurances from the assigned manager that the situation would improve, and they could deliver on their promises, my confidence in their capabilities was significantly diminished.

While grappling with the ghostwriting predicament, I started writing the book myself. I sent them the first chapter and asked them to edit it and make it better. Unfortunately, the edited version I got back was the worst thing I have ever read. They completely butchered my original content but had also painted it in an overwhelmingly negative light. Seeking an outside perspective, I printed out the ten pages for my wife and asked her to read them. My wife is an avid reader and devours several books a week. After she read the material, disheartened, she looked at me and confessed, "I only got through three pages. The grammar is terrible and looks like someone who didn't speak English wrote it. It was absolutely atrocious." This was the final straw; I emailed them and canceled the agreement.

With a money-back guarantee in place, I felt it was worth giving the ghostwriting company a chance initially. Despite my decision to terminate our agreement, the manager begged me for another chance, and offered incentives to continue their services. However, I firmly explained that the language barrier was too much, and the writing style was not what I was looking for. After persistent follow-up calls and emails, they finally agreed to a refund. But weeks went by and the refund never came. I escalated my efforts by sending repeated emails and making several calls. Frustrated by their continued delays, I issued a stern deadline to get the money back. If they didn't send it back, I threatened to post a negative review. Despite their assurances of a swift refund by the following Friday, the deadline came and went with no sign of the reimbursement. Consequently, I proceeded to post a detailed negative review on multiple platforms, highlighting every issue and falsehood I had encountered. The company attempted to have the review taken down by responding to it, but my extensive documentation and evidence prevailed. Low and behold, I got the call that they refunded my money. A year later they reached out, offering to write a complimentary book in exchange for the removal of the review. I stood my ground, emphasizing the importance of transparency regarding their operational practices. While I have often written positive reviews, recognizing outstanding service, I have rarely resorted to negative feedback, reserving it for circumstances where I felt pushed to my limits.

What Would I Change?

The best thing that came out of that debacle is that I ran into a publishing company at an event. Everything happens for a reason, and the debacle of ghostwriting firms led me to where I am at today.

Now back to why I wrote the book—getting on the TEDx stage.

By early 2023, TEDx Boca Raton was coming up. To my surprise, I received a call from the head of the selection committee, expressing an interest in my previous application and requesting a meeting. However, there was a catch—I needed a more compelling topic. Fortunately, I had one that was a huge talking point. Given the prevailing interest in workplace culture amidst the Great Resignation, my TEDx talk was born. My TEDx talk was titled, "How to Stop the Great Resignation with Workplace Culture." And this was all before my book was going to come out. It became evident that I didn't need a book; I needed the right topic to get on that stage.

They loved my topic, and it was time to get ready for the upcoming event. This would be unlike any other speaking engagement I was involved in, requiring me to do something that I had never really done before—I had to practice. Recalling the famous quote, "Practice, we're talking about practice?" from a renowned basketball player, I understood the significance of this often-overlooked aspect. This was not something I was used to. Additionally, the organizers wanted a video of me doing my talk, prompting me to create detailed talking points and a comprehensive slide deck for recording. Upon submission, their feedback was blunt—they deemed the recording unsatisfactory for a Ted Talk.

I made some key mistakes that did not meet the organizer's standards. They advised me to revise the talk and consider getting a speaking coach. I was initially hesitant, but I knew if I was going to be on that stage, I needed to make changes. Despite possessing confidence, I also acknowledge my capacity for learning and improvement. Consequently, I took the initiative to interview a few speaking coaches, and eventually chose Melissa Jacobson, who would best complement my speaking style. Following the advice from the TEDx organizer, I recorded a revised version of my presentation. Melissa viewed both recordings and showed me the difference between the initial and revised versions. I tried to absorb the advice, but I knew I needed further assistance. I was all in at this point, and I wanted to have the best talk of the day. I was going to be on a stage with some people that did great things. I needed to do whatever it takes.

My most pressing challenges revolved around my failure to practice and my tendency to speak too rapidly. With the guidance of my coach, I learned the importance of pacing myself and engaging in regular practice sessions. Having someone to provide me with direction was crucial. I listened attentively and had my talk down pat. I practiced long hours until it was perfected. I rehearsed in front of a mirror, ensuring that I not only memorized the content but also struck the perfect pace. In 2023, the moment arrived. I finally hit the stage and did my Ted talk on the stage at TEDx Boca Raton.

My presentation made an impact on the audience, with several viewers on YouTube proclaiming it as one of the finest talks they had encountered. This experience taught me a crucial lesson—success does not solely hinge on having a book; rather, it revolves around selecting the right topic and effectively reaching the appropriate audience. If you believe, you will achieve. Crush your goals and do not let anyone tell you that you cannot do something. I sincerely hope that this book has inspired you in some way. Now go out and crush your dreams and goals! What will YOU do next?????

Key Lessons from Chapter 9

1. **Embrace challenges as opportunities**: The chapter highlights the author's initial setback of not being selected for a TEDx talk, which ultimately led to the realization that writing a book could be the missing element in achieving this goal. It underscores the importance of reframing setbacks as opportunities for growth and development.

2. **Adaptability and openness to feedback**: The author's willingness to seek a speaking coach and accept constructive criticism regarding their initial video presentation demonstrates the importance of adaptability and receptiveness to feedback in refining one's skills and performance.

3. **Persistence and perseverance**: Despite initial challenges and setbacks, the chapter emphasizes the significance of persistence and perseverance in pursuing one's goals. The author's commitment to refining their speaking skills and perfecting their TEDx talk illustrates the importance of resilience in the face of adversity.

4. **Making informed decisions**: The chapter's account of the author's experience with a ghostwriting firm highlights the importance of making informed decisions when seeking professional assistance, emphasizing the need for thorough research and careful consideration before entering into agreements.

5. **Belief in oneself**: The chapter's underlying message of believing in oneself and one's capabilities underscores the significance of self-confidence and self-assurance in achieving personal and professional success. The author's determination to overcome challenges and deliver an impactful TEDx talk serves as a testament to the power of self-belief and determination.

6. **Continuous practice and preparation**: The chapter emphasizes the importance of continuous practice and preparation in honing one's skills, particularly in the context of public speaking. The author's dedication to practicing their TEDx talk until it was perfected highlights the significance of diligent preparation and rehearsal in delivering a compelling and engaging presentation.

10

Acquisition

Step 1—Acquisition

In the world of business, mergers and acquisitions are a common occurrence, shaping the landscape of industries and companies alike. Some acquisitions are smooth and straightforward, while others are more complex and fraught with challenges. This chapter delves into the intricacies of the Premier Virtual acquisition, highlighting the hurdles and negotiations of the acquisition.

Unbeknownst to many outsiders, the company's software was a true hidden gem in the industry. Its innovative features, scalability, and loyal client base made it a coveted asset for prospective buyers. However, to position the company for acquisition and attract potential investors, the management needed to address some financial concerns and restructure its operations.

The Company's Rise

Premier Virtual was a promising startup with a groundbreaking software solution. The Premier Virtual product gained popularity and built an impressive client database. As I looked at the rise of Premier Virtual and the future, I had to make a decision. The market was getting flooded with competitors, and they were driving the price of the software down. There was also another trend happening, people were forced into the virtual realm when COVID-19 hit, but some wanted to go back to in-person events. We started to see a big shift to hybrid events. There was still a segment of the population that were not technology folks and preferred to get back to in-person gatherings. I liked to say they would rather have an in-person event where they can get a pic to post on social media to show they are doing something than have an online event where the data is right in front of them. Online events give accurate data and in-person can be manipulated. In-person events were not experiencing a resurgence in 2017 but people thought they would suddenly come back. They realized soon enough that an event is only as good as the people running it. People gradually realized that the quality of an event hinges on its organizers. If an event wasn't adequately advertised, if the location wasn't convenient, or if the platform wasn't user-friendly, attendance suffered. And finally, if you don't remind people about the event, attendance could plummet.

Navigating Challenges

Another challenge we ran into was a shift in the marketing and sales team, which we spoke about earlier. We transitioned from a business where leads flowed in daily to a scenario where our team needed to actively pursue business. Despite these challenges, our core team remained dedicated and resourceful. In our quest for a potential sale, I conducted interviews with several investment banking firms, seeking a partner who could guide us through the process. Their perseverance led them to identify potential acquirers who recognized the value of our software and the untapped potential within our client base.

Section 2: The Acquisition Deal

After engaging in several discussions with potential acquirers, Premier Virtual found a compatible suitor. Meeting with companies and their Corporate Development teams was an interesting process. Some valued the software but couldn't figure out how to put it in their portfolio, while others made offers. We walked away with several offers and had to make a decision. Not all were great offers, but some had me set for life. I was not only looking at the money portion of the deal but also the future of Premier Virtual and its team.

Prior to receiving an offer, I met with the CEO of Talent Inc. to go over their proposal. They wanted to show me their vision and how our software fits into their organization. A remarkable aspect of this arrangement was that Premier Virtual would remain an independent company, and our software would find a home within other companies Talent Inc. had acquired, such as Careerminds. These organizations were already established and sought to expand their service offerings and client base. They saw Premier Virtual's software as a strategic asset that could enhance their portfolio and increase their competitiveness.

As in all acquisition deals, it was structured with a mix of cash, rollover equity, and earnout potential.

Rollover Equity: Aligning Interests

As the company explored potential acquisition deals, the management team faced the challenge of structuring a deal that would both entice investors and incentivize key stakeholders. Rollover equity emerged as a viable option, offering the founders the opportunity to roll a portion of their ownership stake into the newly formed entity. This alignment of interests ensured that the founders remained invested in the company's success post-acquisition.

Cash-to-Close: Navigating the Financial Terrain

Acquiring a company and all of their financials poses significant risks for potential buyers. Negotiating a fair cash-to-close arrangement was essential to safeguard the interests of both parties. The company's management worked diligently to present a clear and transparent financial picture, showcasing the potential for growth and profitability. This helped build confidence among potential investors and facilitated an agreement that balanced risk and reward.

Earnout Potential: Bridging the Valuation Gap

Determining the company's precise valuation presented a hurdle in the acquisition process. The earnout structure, a performance-based component of the deal, proved instrumental in bridging the valuation gap. It allowed the company's founders and stakeholders to receive additional payments based on the achievement of specific performance targets post-acquisition. This arrangement reassured the acquiring company that the purchase price would align with the company's actual performance, fostering trust and a shared commitment to future success.

Section 3: Challenges and Strategies

The acquisition process was not without its challenges, and both companies had to overcome various obstacles:

1. **Financial Due Diligence**: Talent Inc. conducted a thorough financial due diligence process to assess the extent of Premier Virtual's financials to determine the appropriate valuation. It required extensive cooperation from the Premier Virtual team to provide the necessary financial data and insights. This is where having a great CFO is key. Bryan was very detailed, and our books were in order. The third-party auditors still ripped it apart. They look for every little thing to see if they could catch something. Everything was in order, but the trends were going in the wrong direction.

2. **Software Due Diligence and Integration**: The third-party software audit couldn't have gone any better. Our Director of IT, Jose, is a documenter and he has files for everything. He sent over all the documentation for them to go over. Next were the calls to see the inner-workings of the system and back end of development. We were supposed to start with three one-hour-long calls to go over the data and then see how much more time once they saw the inner-workings. We had one call, and they said they never saw something documented so much. We passed that audit with flying colors. The next call was with their cyber security, and we passed that as well. Everything on the software side was going great. Integrating the Premier Virtual software into the existing product suite and migrating clients to the new platform required meticulous planning and coordination. Both technical and customer-facing teams had to work closely to ensure a smooth transition.

3. **Cultural Alignment**: The two companies had distinct cultures and merging them successfully was essential for postacquisition collaboration and efficiency. Leadership from both sides emphasized open communication and shared values to create a unified corporate culture.

Section 4: Postacquisition Success

Despite the challenges, the acquisition proved successful for both Premier Virtual and Talent Inc. The infusion of cash enabled Premier Virtual to stabilize its financial situation, and their software integration with offerings expanded the latter's market reach. Premier Virtual stayed as a stand-alone company but their software was integrated into several of the Talent Inc.'s companies that they owned. Talent Inc. got the software they were looking for and Premier Virtual got the database of candidates that they were looking for to really take over the Enterprise marketing and ability to help drive traffic to their clients' events.

The success of the acquisition was a testament to the careful planning, strategic thinking, and perseverance of both companies. It also highlighted the importance of addressing issues transparently and leveraging strengths like innovative software and an established client base to create synergies in the M&A process.

Conclusion

The acquisition journey of Premier Virtual demonstrates that a small company with valuable assets can turn its fortunes around through a well-structured acquisition deal. Rollover equity, cash-to-close, and earnout potential can be powerful tools to align the interests of the parties involved and ensure the success of the combined entity. However, careful consideration of financial, technical, and cultural factors is crucial to overcome challenges and maximize the potential benefits of an acquisition. The case of Premier Virtual serves as an inspiring example of how determination and strategic decision-making can transform a company's destiny.

1. **Importance of addressing market shifts**: The chapter underscores the significance of acknowledging and adapting to market shifts, particularly in relation to changing preferences and trends. The need to recognize evolving customer demands and technological advancements is crucial for sustaining a competitive edge.

2. **Significance of thorough financial and software due diligence**: The chapter highlights the importance of conducting meticulous financial and software due diligence during the acquisition process. It emphasizes the need for comprehensive documentation, transparent financial reporting, and meticulous software auditing to ensure a smooth transition and integration.

3. **Value of cultural alignment in mergers**: The chapter emphasizes the significance of cultural alignment in the context of mergers and acquisitions. It underscores the importance of fostering open communication, shared values, and a unified corporate culture to facilitate postacquisition collaboration and efficiency.

4. **Role of strategic deal structuring**: The chapter emphasizes the role of strategic deal structuring, including the use of rollover equity, cash-to-close arrangements, and earnout potential. It highlights how aligning the interests of both parties and addressing valuation gaps can contribute to the success of the combined entity.

5. **Power of perseverance and strategic decision-making**: The chapter exemplifies the power of perseverance and strategic decision-making in transforming a company's destiny. It underscores the importance of strategic planning, transparent communication, and leveraging strengths to overcome challenges and maximize the potential benefits of an acquisition.

11

A Recap

Reflecting on Growth and Transformation

As I sit down to pen the final chapter of this memoir, it's impossible not to reflect on the journey that has brought me to this point. The path has been winding, filled with unexpected challenges and exhilarating triumphs. From the early days of uncertainty and bootstrap entrepreneurship to the pivotal moments of decision-making and strategic planning, each step has contributed to the evolution of not just a company but of an individual. In this chapter, I aim to delve deeper into the lessons learned, the evolution of strategies, and the vision for the future that has been shaped by the experiences shared in the preceding chapters.

Embracing Entrepreneurial Spirit

The story of Premier Virtual's inception and the challenges encountered along the way serves as a testament to the power of entrepreneurial spirit. The early days were marked by relentless determination and the willingness to take risks in pursuit of a dream. The struggles and setbacks encountered in the initial stages became the building blocks of resilience and adaptability. The significance of fostering an environment that nurtures innovation and fosters a culture of perseverance has been a defining factor in the company's growth trajectory.

The journey of entrepreneurship is often glamorized, with the spotlight focused on the success stories and the triumphs. However, often remaining hidden are the countless moments of self-doubt, the sleepless nights spent pondering the next move, and the unwavering determination required to overcome the seemingly insurmountable hurdles. Premier Virtual's journey embodies the essence of this struggle, serving as a beacon of hope for all those embarking on their entrepreneurial quests.

Navigating the Competitive Landscape

The competitive landscape within the tech industry has always been dynamic and fiercely challenging. Adapting to the ever-evolving trends and shifts in consumer preferences has been crucial in maintaining a competitive edge. The exploration of hybrid events in response to the changing market demands marked a strategic move, showcasing the company's ability to anticipate industry trends and pivot accordingly. Understanding the importance of market positioning and the necessity of staying ahead of the curve has been a pivotal lesson in the journey.

In an industry characterized by rapid advancements and disruptive innovations, complacency is the enemy of progress. The ability to continuously assess market trends, identify emerging opportunities, and pivot strategies accordingly has been instrumental in Premier Virtual's sustained growth and relevance. The journey has underscored the importance of fostering a culture of adaptability and continuous learning, allowing the company to stay ahead of the competition and carve a distinct niche within the competitive landscape.

Leadership Insights and Team-Building

Leading a company through various stages of growth requires a nuanced understanding of effective leadership and team-building strategies. The challenges faced in transitioning from a lead-flow model to actively pursuing business highlighted the significance of fostering a dynamic and proactive sales and marketing team. Emphasizing the importance of effective communication, fostering a culture of collaboration, and empowering team members to take ownership were pivotal in navigating the company through its transitional phases.

The journey of Premier Virtual has been characterized by the unwavering dedication of its team members, each contributing their unique talents and expertise to the collective success of the company. The importance of nurturing a culture of trust, transparency, and mutual respect has been instrumental in fostering a collaborative environment where each team member feels valued and empowered. The leadership insights gained from the journey have emphasized the significance of cultivating a shared vision, fostering open communication, and leading by example to inspire the best in every individual.

Strategic Partnerships and Collaborations

The journey of Premier Virtual has been shaped by the strategic partnerships and collaborations that have played a crucial role in the company's expansion. The significance of identifying compatible suitor companies during the acquisition process highlighted the importance of aligning organizational values and long-term visions. The complexities involved in navigating acquisition deals underscored the importance of carefully structured agreements that align the interests of stakeholders and ensure the company's sustained growth.

In the intricate web of business collaborations and strategic partnerships, the ability to identify mutually beneficial opportunities and cultivate meaningful relationships has been key to Premier Virtual's journey. The successful integration of acquired companies, the alignment of shared values, and the leveraging of complementary strengths have all contributed to the company's continued success and market relevance. The journey has illuminated the transformative power of strategic partnerships in fostering innovation, expanding market reach, and creating synergies that drive sustainable growth and development.

Transformative Growth and Resilience

The challenges encountered during the acquisition process, ranging from financial due diligence to software integration and cultural alignment, served as opportunities for transformative growth and resilience. The successful navigation of these obstacles demonstrated the company's ability to adapt, innovate, and emerge stronger from adversity. Leveraging the strengths of innovative software solutions and an established client base played a crucial role in the postacquisition success and solidified the company's position within the industry.

The journey of Premier Virtual serves as a testament to the transformative power of resilience, adaptability, and strategic decision-making. The ability to weather storms, overcome obstacles, and emerge stronger on the other side has been pivotal in defining the company's legacy and setting the stage for future growth and expansion. The lessons learned from the journey have underscored the importance of fostering a culture of innovation, embracing change, and leveraging challenges as opportunities for transformative growth and development.

The Journey Ahead

As I look back on the experiences shared throughout these chapters, I am reminded of the transformative power of determination, strategic decision-making, and unwavering commitment to excellence. The lessons learned, the challenges overcome, and the successes celebrated have all contributed to shaping a vision for the future. The journey of Premier Virtual serves as a testament to the limitless potential that lies within the realms of entrepreneurial spirit and the power of strategic partnerships. As the company continues to evolve and adapt in the ever-changing landscape of the tech industry, the vision remains clear: to innovate, inspire, and continue pushing the boundaries of what is possible.

A Call to Action

To all the aspiring entrepreneurs, innovators, and visionaries reading this memoir, I leave you with a call to action. Embrace the challenges, learn from the setbacks, and never lose sight of your vision. Stay true to your values, nurture your team, and build strategic partnerships that will elevate your journey to new heights. Remember, the path to success is not always linear, but it is the resilience, adaptability, and unwavering determination that will ultimately define your legacy in the world of business and beyond.

12

A Final Note—Social, Ethical, and Moral Considerations

1. Transparency and Honesty: Upholding a commitment to transparency and honesty in all interactions with VC teams, including providing accurate and comprehensive information about the company's financial health, operational strategies, and potential risks. Establishing open communication channels and disclosing pertinent information in a timely and forthright manner are crucial for building trust and credibility.

Example: Providing accurate financial projections and operational challenges to the VC team laid the groundwork for building trust and credibility in business relationships.

2. Fair and Equitable Negotiations: Striving to engage in fair and equitable negotiations that prioritize the interests of all stakeholders involved. This involves conducting thorough due diligence, assessing the terms of the agreement from a long-term perspective, and ensuring that the negotiated terms align with the company's values and strategic objectives.

Example: Ensuring fair and equitable negotiations with business partners, reflected the author's commitment to fostering mutually beneficial partnerships and maintaining a sense of fairness in all business dealings.

3. Ethical Decision-Making: Adhering to ethical decision-making frameworks that consider the impact of various choices on not only the company's financial success but also its employees, customers, and the broader community. Balancing the pursuit of profitability with a commitment to ethical business practices, environmental sustainability, and social responsibility is imperative for fostering a positive corporate culture and contributing to the greater good.

Example: Prioritizing employee welfare over firing everyone and maximizing profits during a challenging financial period underscored the author's ethical approach to business management and the prioritization of employee well-being.

4. Accountable Corporate Governance: Establishing robust corporate governance practices that emphasize accountability, risk management, and compliance with regulatory standards. Implementing effective oversight mechanisms, conducting regular audits, and adhering to industry best practices are essential for ensuring that the company operates ethically and upholds its commitment to stakeholders.

Example: Implementing rigorous auditing practices and compliance measures within the company, demonstrated the author's dedication to accountability and responsible corporate governance, ensuring adherence to regulatory standards and mitigating potential risks.

5. Social Impact and Community Engagement: Integrating social impact initiatives and community engagement programs into the company's core business strategies. Investing in corporate social responsibility programs, supporting local communities, and championing diversity and inclusion initiatives can contribute to building a positive brand reputation and fostering meaningful connections with the broader society.

Example: Partnering with local schools and community organizations to promote STEM education and support underprivileged students, demonstrated the author's dedication to making a positive social impact and contributing to the betterment of the community.

By adhering to these ethical and social responsibilities, a corporation can foster a culture of integrity, trust, and sustainability within the company while simultaneously establishing a positive reputation within the VC community and the broader business landscape.

These responsibilities serve as guiding principles for ethical decision-making and underscore commitment to conducting business in a manner that aligns with the values of transparency, accountability, and social impact.

Extra: The TEDx Transcript

One of the primary motivations behind writing my book was to secure a spot on the TEDx stage. After my initial applications were rejected, I noticed that the selected speakers were all authors, which clarified my next steps. While writing the book, I submitted another application to TEDx Boca Raton and was selected to speak, achieving my goal even before becoming an author. This experience taught me that the selection criteria focused more on having a compelling idea to share rather than merely being an eloquent speaker. Below, you'll find a transcript of my talk. You can also watch it on YouTube by searching for "TEDx Steve Edwards."

America, we have a problem. We do. We have lots of them, but the great resignation is here. But how do we solve the great resignation? How do we get employees to not quit? Culture is very easy to sense, but you know what? It's hard to measure. How do you measure culture? Here are some stats that when I saw these are just crazy. There are 360 million people in the United States, 160 million in the workforce. And before I give you this next answer, I want you to put a number into your head for me. How many people quit their jobs in 2022? Think about that for a second. How many people quit their jobs in 2022?

Over 50 million people quit their jobs. Who thought it was going to be that high? Probably not a lot of people. Almost a third of America quit their jobs and the year before, we had 47 million people quit their jobs. We talked about the great resignation happened in 2020, but guess what? It happened in 2022. All those people that quit their jobs in 2020 that thought the grass was greener on the other side, "We're going to go, we're getting our life back. We're going to go remote. We're getting all these things back." Guess what they realized, the grass wasn't greener. Do you know where the grass is greenest? Where you water it. So a lot of these people are making these decisions to come back. Now, why is culture so important? Richard

Branson talks about it and he's been talking about it for years. There's a couple of quotes up here by Richard Branson, but my favorite one is, "Your customers don't come first. Your employees come first. Take care of your employees and they'll take care of your customers."

So think about that, right? How do I build this culture? How do I impact on this culture within my organization so that people want to come to work, that people want to be excited, right? He talks about how when you build that culture that's there and people want to come to work, you're going to get better talent. We could talk about all the things that positive workplace culture helps with, better retention, better recruiting, better morale. Those are all things that are important. There's a *Harvard Business Review* and there are so many articles, so many studies out there about culture, but one of my favorite ones is Denise Lee Yohn. She talked about workplace culture is everybody's job. Now, I like to call it the old school versus the new school of employer culture.

It used to be the CEO would go down to the HR department and say, "Hey, we want to get a pulse on what's going on. We want to know what's going on within the company." So what do they do? The HR company sends out a survey. Now, before that survey, what happens at a lot of larger companies and some smaller companies, they have company trips, right? "Oh, we're going to have a company trip. It's so exciting. We're going to go to Hawaii, wherever we're going to go." But who gets to go to those? The top salespeople. The top executives. What about that secretary? What about that warehouse worker? They don't get to go on these trips, so they may not love the culture. But you know what? The top-level executive went, "Man, I go to Hawaii every year. I go to Fiji, I go to The Bahamas."

Yes, they love it. So they look at this survey at the end and they say, "Oh, okay, we got a little bit on our plate here." What I like to say is they can create a culture team. And what is a culture team? A culture team is taking a diverse group of individuals within your organization. Some low level, some medium level, different races, different religions, single, married, with kids, not with kids. When I first graduated college, I always wanted the happy hours, the party, and that was what I thought was the company that I wanted. Now with a wife and two kids, I'd rather have a weekend barbecue, right? Culture's changed. But having this culture team and being able to put this together so they can say, what can we do within the organization to really have your pulse on it? Instead of going top down, which the old school message was, let's go bottom up.

Let's get the people in the bottom to say, "What can we do to help?" Who remembers a big wheel when they were a kid? We had a lot of them, right? You might think I'm crazy here. A lot of people do. Wouldn't be the first and won't be the last time. But I look at business like a big wheel. You take that center console and that seat, that base of that big wheel, that's your operations team. That's your IT, your finance, your accounting, your HR, your customer service. That's the base of your company. That big front wheel, that's your sales team, right? That's what's generating the revenue for your company. It's there. Those pedals, that's your marketing team, that's your branding. That's what's helping get your company forward. They're working together, right? Sales and marketing working together to really get your brand out, to get your organization out. Those handlebars, that's your leadership. That's steering the company. That's the one that comes in and helps pivot your organization where they need to go.

Now, those back wheels, those back wheels are your employee experience, your workplace culture. And to me, that's one of the biggest impacts on your organization. Now, if I take any of the other things away, the handlebars, the tire, that base, that big wheel is going to fall apart and so is the business. It's not going to run smoothly. Now, I could take those tires off, I can take that workplace culture and make it crap, and your business is still going to go forward, but it's going to go slow. There's going to be friction. It's not going to be a smooth process out there. You put those back on, your company gets back running. So, think of this. Every time now you see a big wheel, you're going to picture each one of these things and say, "That is like a business."

Right now there's a lot of talk about AI and who's scared of AI. AI is here. It's coming to fruition. And if you think about AI really, if you look at AI and the worker shortage, it's going to come over the next few years, AI can play a role in a positive thing. There's challenges to it, but there's also a lot of positive things that can come out of here. So when you're thinking that AI is going to be a threat, it's not. It's going to help the worker shortage and help other things. Now, you can't be scared of AI. And I'm going to tell you a little story about me being scared. In 1995, I was standing a thousand feet in the air looking out the door of a C-130. I was 18 years old. I was in airborne school. I was about to be the first jump out of an airplane.

Now I'm scared of heights. I hate heights, but I believe sometimes you got to do things that you don't want to do. So I'm standing in the door, I got my parachute on my back and I was the door guy. So I'm standing there, jump master looks at me, probably knew where I was at because I was scared. I was shaking, I was sweating. He goes, "Are you scared?" I go, "Hell yeah, I'm scared jump master." And he goes,

"Look at the ground, tell them you ain't scared." I go, "I'm not scared of you." Quick glance, he goes, "I told you to look at the ground." He's screaming at me. And I'm like, "I'm not scared of you," shaking, sweating. Next thing you hear, it was, "Green light go, green light go." I step out into nothing hoping my parachute would open. Now it did, obviously, because I'm here, but I stepped out.

I wasn't scared. I did something that I wasn't comfortable with and I jumped out into nothing. And that's how we have to look at AI. Don't be scared of it. Embrace it, because guess what? It's here to stay. It is here, here, here. Now I want to talk about a human factor, but before I do that, I want to tell a story. About 2017, I got recruited from one of my clients. It was a pinnacle of my career. I got offered a job, US$250,000 base salary. I made US$8,000 a year when I was in the army. So, do the math, I was pretty happy. I was going to be number two in the company under the president. I was running the training, recruiting, and sales teams. It was my ideal dream job, my dream salary, company full benefits, company card, company credit card. They were a US$30 million company and wanted to go to US$100 million company. And I was going to get a bonus for that.

I was set. I was excited. Take the job. I get up there the first weekend, owner of the company whom I'd never met before, comes in and he goes, first thing he says is, "You motherf'ers, I'm going to fire you if you don't do this." I was like, "Ooh, that was an interesting way to enter a sales meeting." I've never heard so many F-bombs. And again, I was in the 82nd Airborne Division. So I jumped out of airplanes and I never heard so many F-bombs in a sales meeting. So I then go, "All right, this is interesting, right? Different things." But after a couple of months, my morals, my ethics, the way that they had this toxic culture just was not me. It wasn't who I was. So then I went home one weekend and I told my wife, "I don't think this is going to be good. I think I'm going to leave." She's like, "The money. This is your dream. You got everything you want."

I go, "I don't have happiness. That's not who I am. I can't do it." I went in that Monday, I parted ways, but I always said, "I will never build a toxic culture like that." And I said, "When I build my organization, it will never be like that." And I believe the human culture, the human touches, being able to sit down with my employees on a monthly basis and talk about life. And I actually had one of my employees bring that to me, and we had a good culture. And he said, "Why don't you do this?" And it was a game changer because now they get to see me as a human and I get to see them as a human. So what I'm going to tell you here is my action item. Build a culture team, build it, be involved, know who your teams are. Every single person in here can impact it by creating your culture. Are you just going to live it or are you going to talk about it? Make an impact. Live it. Don't just talk about it.

Meet the Author

Steve Edwards, hailing from Chippewa Falls, Wisconsin, distinguished himself in the elite 82nd Airborne Division after high school. Transitioning to FAU, he honed his sales expertise, driven by a pursuit of financial success. In 2018, recognizing a decline in engagement at in-person hiring events, he founded Premier Virtual, revolutionizing the industry with innovative virtual solutions.

A renowned speaker on workforce culture and talent retention, Steve's leadership led Premier Virtual to be repeatedly recognized as a top Florida workplace. A TEDx speaker and successful entrepreneur, he transitioned his business from concept to acquisition in just four years. Dedicated to his family, Steve is also a devoted husband to Christine and a loving father to two boys, Tristan and Gavin, embodying the ethos of 'family first.' Hosting the podcast "Weeding Through the BS," he continues to foster meaningful conversations on critical professional and personal topics.